STEP STEP JUMP

STEP STEP JUMP

Transforming Trauma to Triumph from the 46th Floor

By

ANNABEL QUINTERO M.ED.

Step Step Jump: Transforming Trauma to Triumph from the 46th Floor
Published by Runa Publishing
Seattle, Washington, U.S.A.
Copyright ©2021 ANNABEL QUINTERO. All rights reserved.

QUINTERO, ANNABEL, Author
STEP STEP JUMP
ANNABEL QUINTERO
ISBN: 978-1-7370051-0-0 (paperback)
ISBN: 978-1-7370051-1-7 (hardcover)
Edited by: Ashley Rappa; www.humanwritesconsulting.com
Photographer credit: John Curry; www.johncurryphotography.net
Book cover design by: Rick Penn-Kraus; www.RPKdesigns.com
Interior design: Tanya Brockett; www.HallagenInk.com

QUANTITY PURCHASES: Schools, companies, professional groups, clubs, and other organizations may qualify for special terms when ordering quantities of this title. For information, email Runa Publishing at info@runapublishing.com.

This book is printed in the United States of America.

To all the beautiful souls who shaped me:

for raising me to be honest, just, and loving - Ruben, Nancy, Shirley, Norma, Johanna, Paul & Carol, and my extended family,

my group of soul purposeful women, who always encourage me,

Lisa Nichols and the loving tribe I am a part of, thank you for your endless support

----

To my hearts:

Sophia and Selene, my two goddesses

who teach me & love me and give me

purpose everyday

To those who are

going through their own life altering moment

Contents

1   Shattered Glass   1

2   In All My Wildest Dreams   27

3   The September Fall   43

4   Church Street Smoke   57

5   Saint Anthony   71

6   Heaven and Earth Collide   81

7   My Brother's Keeper   97

8   In the Flow   113

9   Home Unbound   121

10   Unsettled Hearts   137

11   Trees and Mountains   155

12   Mother Earth   169

13   A New New York   183

     Epilogue   199

     Acknowledgements   207

     Further Readings   211

     About the Author   213

Shattered Glass

I looked up and was greeted by the New York City skyline. I could feel the energy radiating from the streets, could almost hear the sounds of Manhattan waking up with me. I reached up to touch the outline of the buildings against the blue, my fingers tracing the point of the Empire State Building, the art deco outlines of the Chrysler Building, the two matching blocks of the Twin Towers that stood just taller than the rest—the World Trade Center.

I knew I would live there someday. But what I could never could have known was that just a handful of years later, those buildings would be set aflame as I struggled to breathe on the 42nd floor. That soon after, they would be knocked clear out of the sky, reduced to rubble, cracking open my heart and forever changing the course of my life.

But then, just a high school kid, that majestic city in two dimensions on the wall of my bedroom was the most beautiful thing I could imagine, a beacon of hope that beckoned to me.

From down the hall, I heard my father's voice.

"Annabel, I hope you're ready! You've got a flight to catch!"

I was a high school student, the daughter of Ecuadorian immigrants, a brown-skinned girl in a light-skinned world, but I already had big dreams.

"Your mother will be here any minute!" my dad said.

My eyes snapped back to the Big Apple, and a thrill ran through me. Who knew what incredible things awaited me in the place I so longed to call home? Who knew what I could become in a city so full of dreams that it is said to never truly sleep?

I reached my hand up again to touch the steel of the skyline. "Be right there!" I yelled down to my father, never taking my eyes off Manhattan. "Be right there," I said again, softer this time, as though I could will myself across the country. It was a proclamation to the powers that be. It was a promise to myself.

The first time I had ever seen New York City in person was in the spring of 1991. My cousin Fernando was getting married, and he had grown up in New Jersey. I was entering my senior year of high school and hadn't ventured very far from home.

"It will be good for you to see some of the world," my mother had said, and we were soon on a plane to the Garden State to stay with my Tio Galo and Tia Kira.

Fernando's was a sweet wedding in a small suburban town. Since most of our Latino family wasn't local, the bride's Anglo-Saxon friends and relatives filled the whole reception. My mom and Tia were there to celebrate in every way, and in my family, a wedding wasn't complete without dancing. But only rock music pumped through the speakers, so they stayed off the dance floor, waiting, hoping to hear something familiar, something Latin. Finally, after several hours and several glasses of champagne, a Nirvana song came on.

My mother stood up and stated loudly: "*Bueno no voy a esperar mas, si solo van a tocar rock n roll entonces voy a bailarlo y gozarme.*"

Translation: "Well, I'm not going to wait any longer! If they're only going to play rock, then I'm going to dance anyway and enjoy myself."

It wasn't Latino, but it was a Seattle band, which ended up being enough.

I knew I couldn't miss this, so I went with her onto the dance floor. The opening bars of "Teen Spirit" gave way to the hardcore chorus, and the two of us used every inch of our bodies to dance along. Everyone was shocked! Maybe these people didn't know how to dance? All they seemed to know how to do was to choke on their drinks as they watched us, their mouths and eyes wide.

Even my cousin Fernando was surprised, watching his aunt make her black velvet dress do things it had never done before. Tia Kira joined in, and the three of us riffed along with the ripping guitar, getting into our own grunge groove.

The following day, our bodies sore but our hearts happy, Tio Galo drove us to the city, and I was mesmerized by the sheer size of it, so much bigger than could ever be captured in the poster on my bedroom wall at home. The buildings rose like giants in the sky. Driving past these iconic structures was a powerful precession that felt like a rite of passage block by block.

So many of my family members had started their lives in America in New York before migrating to Seattle, so even as I was overwhelmed by so much of what I saw, it also felt as if part of it was in my blood. I grew up looking at photos of my mom and my aunt when they were in their 20s—young, free, single, newly arrived immigrants in a formidable city, posing together on rooftops.

Tio Galo had us making our way to the fashion district via the Lincoln Tunnel, and I couldn't believe the factories, the people, all the stores and buildings. People walking their dogs, people shopping, people delivering goods, everyone working, working, working. I had never before seen so much concentrated focus on the daily grind.

"Another day, another dollar." Tio Galo said when I mentioned it. "So, where do you all want to go? *You're* not working today—where should we go?"

"I want to eat some real New York pizza," said my mom. "Let's just stay in Midtown; maybe we can walk down 42nd Street and go to where we used to watch movies."

And we did just that, but it wasn't like she had remembered it from her time there in the 1960s. It was gritty, grimy, studded with strip clubs and the seedier side of city life. But we did find a pizza place, where we devoured what was available only after tossing aside each one of the slimy canned mushrooms that had been thoughtlessly dumped on top. It was still good, a true testament to the baked-in appeal of a New York slice.

We walked around the city at a leisurely pace, making our way downtown as my mom and Tia talked about all the boys they dated, the men who used to court them, the adventures they got up to in their youth.

A mall had just been built on 34th Street, and it was the biggest, most beautiful shopping center I'd ever seen. It made even the most cutting-edge malls back home in Seattle look like miniature facsimiles. We then walked to Macy's, and my 17-year-old eyes couldn't believe it—it was the size of a whole city block, big and grand, with escalators made of wood and price tags with bigger numbers on them than I'd ever seen before.

Yet the biggest thing that struck me wasn't the size of this brick building, of any of these brick buildings; it was a shift in my own spirit. I felt alive in a way that I hadn't ever felt before, like my entire frequency of being had been turned all the way up. I had always heard stories from my parents about life in the city, about how much they loved the energy and the rhythm of things.

My father had moved to New York from Ecuador, determined to fulfill his desire to build a life and start a family in the United States he'd always imagined. When he came to New York, it was intoxicating, but it was nothing like the trees and mountains he had for so long yearned to call home. So he found a way out west—to Walla Walla, Washington, a small town with an Adventist College where he could study. He had always been a spiritual man, but never religious, but the college offered him a way to the cedars of his dreams.

But at that moment, I knew with every beat of my young heart that this city would be the start of my own story. We left that night, and I couldn't wait to come back.

I hatched a plan. I would combine my new favorite place on the planet with all of my biggest dreams—becoming a model, a dancer, and a fashion designer. I knew New York was my city, the place where I would live out my dreams and soar. All I had to do was plot the course, and I had every confidence that my hopes would turn into reality.

"I want to be a model, dad," I said in the backyard when I got back from my trip, full of confidence and candor. My stepmom Shirley and stepsister Holly were there, all of us eating lunch and relaxing outside.

He scoffed. "How are you going to feed yourself, Annabel? You have to think of the bigger picture."

"I *am* thinking of the bigger picture. This is what I want to do. It's so clear to me that this is what I'm meant for."

But he only shook his head.

"You are meant to study hard and get good grades so you can get a scholarship. Or, of course, the Army is another option. I don't advise you to do the latter, but it's your choice," he said with unwavering eyes. "You are the only one of your siblings who has ever gone to private school. You know your mother and I can't afford to pay for college, but with all As on your transcript, you can get a scholarship and go to a great university."

"I know that's what you want, dad. But I want to dance. I want to design beautiful clothes. I want to be a model."

It took so much courage to say this to him, to voice my deepest hopes out loud for him and the world to hear. Saying it meant I really wanted it, and really wanting it meant I had a responsibility to go after it.

"*Model?*" he asked, incredulously, frustrated by my perceived lack of practicality. "You don't have the body for modeling."

I looked down at myself. I still had child-like curves, and my stomach had always had a mind of its own.

"I won't always be this size, dad. I am working out all the time, and I know it's what I want to do."

"*Modeling?* Holly has the body for modeling, not you," he said matter-of-factly, gesturing over to where she sat, reading a magazine.

My stepmom came to my defense.

"Honey!" she yelled, looking at him sternly. "If she wants to model, let her model. That's her dream, and it's her life."

"All I'm saying is that dreams are in your mind, and she's going to have to actually put in a lot of hard work to get where she needs to be."

I know I should have been offended, that the words should have cut to the bone, but I knew him. He wasn't the kind of person who would offer support no matter what, but he would always show up with what made sense, what was practical and secure. It was an immigrant sensibility, prioritizing safety and minimizing risk at every turn.

In many ways, he was right, and I knew it. But I also knew what was right for me. In a perfect world, I could have both—the ease and the fulfillment, the security and the satisfaction of achieving what I'd always wanted.

And so, I attempted to pursue two paths. After graduating from one of the best private high schools in the state, I went to Shoreline Community College just north of Seattle to save money and stay close to home. I was paying my own way, so I took the practical approach, but I ended up loving my time there.

I met so many amazing friends—Sunny, Mohammed, Sultan, Angkea, and Steve—and by the winter quarter, I really wanted to move out of my dad's house. Claire, my best friend at the time, was going to Seattle University and asked if I could dorm with her. Her school was right down the street from mine, so I inquired to see if it was possible for a community college student to live in the Seattle University dorms, and fortunately for me, it was.

Claire was very supportive of my dreams, and my sophomore year in college was a year like no other up to that point. I took amazing classes that taught me so much about history, culture, politics, and people. I lived in the dormitory at Seattle University and walked everywhere. I had professors of color for the first time, the student body was diverse, and I was in Capitol Hill, which truly embraced diversity in all forms. My student life was further enriched by being the president of ADELA, the Asociación de Estudiantes Latino Americanos. Through my studies and by connecting with others, I truly learned the political history that created the conditions in which my identity was shaped: the why, how, and what it means to be African, Native American, and European, and how all three rolled together to create and inform my Latino identity.

But by the end of my sophomore year, I was ready for more. My sights, as always, were set on New York, so I called my brother Paul, a student at Columbia University who was finishing up his master's degree in business.

"Hey, Schnannabel," he said, picking up on the first ring.

I didn't wait for him to ask why I was calling, the idea of small talk was unbearable, so I just blurted out, "Do you think I should move to Manhattan to go to school?"

"Manhattan is expensive," he replied without missing a beat. "And NYC isn't a city to study in. It's not like any other city; there are too many people, too many distractions. It's a city built for being out and about, not buried in a book. Do what I did instead and get your bachelor's degree, keep your debt low, and come to the city ready to really work and live."

"I feel so stuck," I sighed. "I want to be a business major, but there are too many prerequisites. If I stay in school to finish those, I feel like I may never get to New York."

"Why do you need a business degree?"

"To become a banker. I know it's practical, but I do have a passion for it. I don't want to just make money, I want to harness the power of the markets to really make a change." *And dad would approve,* I thought.

"You don't need a business major to be a banker. Most of the bankers I know majored in something else entirely. This is your one shot at studying what you love; then, you can spend the rest of your life working hard. You'll make it just fine."

"Well, I do love politics."

"If you love politics, Washington is the place to live. New York is the financial center. But no matter what, politics and money go hand in hand."

Something deep inside me tugged at the edges of my mind as if to say *don't forget about me.*

"Of course, I love the arts, too," I added, torn by the many sides of my brain vying for attention.

"My sister, the starving artist. Didn't we struggle enough growing up?" I could tell he was smiling, though, shaking his head as though willing me to clear my own.

So, I once again split the difference between what I wanted and what I thought I should do. In 1995, after receiving my associate degree, I applied to the Fashion Institute of Technology on 27th Street in Manhattan and the University of Washington in Seattle. A few months after I submitted my applications, I received the official word: I had been accepted to both. I was thrilled! But my elation was soon followed by a disappointment that was hard to swallow: FIT didn't offer any financial aid, which meant I'd have to pay tuition and housing in New York all on my own, which just wasn't in the current cards for me.

With a heavy heart, I accepted the offer from UW and transferred there. I was assigned student housing, and when I opened the envelope to find out my future address, I couldn't help but smile: my shared student apartment was located on Brooklyn Street. I may have had to give up on my New York dreams for the immediate future, but New York hadn't given up on me.

In the spring of 1995, I met Fever. I had first seen him years earlier after a high school party—it was almost like a cliché, where we locked eyes as he crossed a parking lot, and the rest of the world fell away. Although nothing happened back then, and even though I thought I'd never see him again, there was something about his energy that I hadn't been able to forget.

It felt a bit like fate, then, when I rounded a corner and saw him standing there in front of the dining hall in his shiny white Yankees jacket and jeans. He looked up as I looked over, and the effect was instant—the edges of my vision blurred out. There was only him.

We started dating, and the world changed. Fever was a break dancer (b-boy) and he opened up corners of the city and myself that I never knew existed before. I promised I would teach him salsa if he would teach me to break. Breakin' came first.

Fever was part of a hip-hop crew called Droppin Vicious Styles (DVS) that was central to the Seattle hip-hop scene. We'd stay up late watching old VHS tapes of 1980s breakin' footage, and even though I remembered so many of those videos from growing up, I had no idea that hip-hop was more than the urban setting, more than fashion or a dance, that it was a culture, a mindset, a community.

Though I had grown up dancing wherever and however I could, it wasn't until I learned how to break that I learned what my body was truly capable of. Fever took me to Jefferson Community Center, a hotspot for hip-hop, when we walked in there I met DV One, one of the program managers, I was introduced to Danny and Ryan who were getting up in their black books with Sneke and this whole group of Asian and Pacific islander youth called the Boss crew. Fever then introduced me to a kid who was just starting to learn to dance. He was a really good soccer player, and his athleticism was an asset. I felt my own muscles subtly contract as I shook his hand—we both had fire in our bellies and humbled hearts to learn.

"This is Jerome," said Fever.

We nodded to one another.

"I'm going to show you both some basics to get you started. Everyone wants to do the power moves, the windmills and head spins, but the foundation is in the flavor of your top rocks and footwork, then you can add drops, taps, CCs, and power moves," Fever explained. "Learn the fundamentals first, and your own flavor and style will just come out over time. Every dance form has a clear format, a blueprint. Once you learn the blueprint, you can add on from there, but the two most important things to learn first are the top rock and the footwork."

To demonstrate, he knelt down onto the balls of his feet, keeping his torso straight, then shifted his weight from side to side. Once we could do that simple more, which depended on flexibility, he really got started, leaning on his right arm, then on his left. Luckily, I was pretty flexible.

"Now I'm going to teach you basic footwork. One, two, three, four, imagine there are four main corners of a box but six footsteps; these are the core movements," said Fever. He stepped and stepped, and then he just kept going faster and faster, blazing through the steps before he cut a freeze and stood up.

"Don't get caught up in the hype, in the moves that look good—some people have no rhythm. They aren't dancing and expanding the culture; they're just bustin' out power moves to be acrobatic. The basics, top rocks and footwork, that's where you both need to begin. Now it's your turn."

Jerome and I just looked at each other, eyes wide and hearts pounding. And then we hit the floor. We ripped it up, full of energy and enthusiasm. I picked it up quickly, but I heard Soulone yelling, "Pick up that ass!" and Fever saying, "Hold your chest up, don't face the floor so much." All I could do was smile and laugh at myself. The next day, it felt like I'd run marathons, plural, I was so sore, my body so heavy, everything stretched to the max.

The following week, I went to Art Bar for the first time. Every Tuesday night, it was "The Foundation" on 2nd and Pike. We passed security with a nod from Alonzo and walked into a sea of velvet red drapes and curtains, brick walls, and antique furniture lining the edges of the room. There were people on the right, people on the left, a bar, and the dance floor right in the middle. This was where the action was—this sultry, afro-centric mélange of culture with body movements that poured like liquid. The sound was so clear, so deep and profound.

It was also my first night seeing some of the superstars of the scene. Source of Labor was gettin' down, DJ Kamikaze was spinning, Wordsayer and Negus1 were the emcees, and Kutfather would bring that bombastic sound. It was humbling, awe-inspiring to experience real underground hip-hop culture. Up to that point, I hadn't physically been in the same space as an emcee in full flow, to feel and see it, to hear the rhyme in a vibe of creation, acting as the doorway of lyrical sound to our souls.

The deejay would spin familiar classics along with some new songs, then blend the two into a melody never heard before. You would hear real hip hop and gangster, X Clan and Nas, and so much more. The collective consciousness was living its full potential by coming together weekly like a secret club meeting and generating pure art from that moment of love, inspiration, and struggle.

Most of the movers and shakers were just being themselves in an expression of art and culture all wrapped up in the term hip hop, but they were all there, all of Seattle's best and brightest hip-hop stars. The deejays would rotate records, and you'd be in the presence of legends like B-Mello, Supreme, DV One, Pryme Tyme, and Soul One. On the mic, you'd hear Shane, Jake One, and Vitamin D speaking before the ladies—Beyond Reality, Peace of Soul, and Kylea "Eryka White"—rotated in with their own flavor. All the emcees—Damian, Stack, and Samson— were hanging out with Rob Nice of the L Brothers. Devon, Top Spin, and my dear friends, Rainbow, Audrise, Jojo, and her bestie Carlisia, were there, too. If you were in the hip-hop scene in the late '90s, Art Bar was the place.

Fever and his crew were the best of the best teachers. Hip hop has four main elements: b-boyin'/b-girlin', writing (graffiti art-bubble letters, wild style, top to bottoms), emcee (rapping), and DeeJay'ing (scratching, mixing, and beat juggling). Our crew was mostly made up of writers, but we would also break. Our core members were Fever, Supreme, the DJ and collector; Sneke, a writer and breaker; Hews, Went and Rey One, three writers; and SoulOne, who could do it all: break, write, deejay and emcee.

I was overwhelmed with the vibe, the culture, the creativity of it all. There was so much talent in that building and in that community, but it was also truly a family, and I was welcomed home with open hearts and minds by each and all. Something stirred within me, a reverence and an awakening of experiencing the world in a new way.

It was a wonderful time. By night, I'd be living a hip-hop dynasty dream, and by day, I was a senior in college. I had already taken all my hardcore classes, so my senior year was mostly the electives I hadn't taken because I had my nose to the grindstone in my first few years. I was also working part-time as a program manager at Seattle Central Community College, helping teachers get their ESL credentials so they could better serve students who didn't speak English as a first language. It was good work, and I loved the mission, but it was also my first office job and not without its struggles.

To get to work, I jumped on the bus and headed to Capitol Hill. I always loved taking the bus because I could sit and look out the window and enjoy the view. I especially loved the area by Montlake Bridge. It was so sweet, so quaint, and I loved the building structure and the bright little green belts along the water.

But that feeling of serenity would disappear as soon as I walked into the office. The second I sat down, the director would knock at my door and yell a bunch of directives at me. He was a hothead who almost always smelled like alcohol, and no matter what I did, he never seemed satisfied with my job performance. There was always something wrong, always something else I had to do, always something I didn't do enough of.

Most of the time, I'd smile and nod and try to focus on the good. I had my own office! It was my first real, full-time job, and I got to help people learn.

I especially loved that part of it, and the feeling of accomplishment was often enough to get me through the difficult moments. If life was all about balance, then the counterweight to my office job was the hip-hop scene. Without my nights at Jefferson and Art Bar, without my crew and Fever, I couldn't have gotten through the days filled with files and phone calls.

I was grateful for the good, but in the quiet moments when I'd listen deeply to myself, I still knew something wasn't fully aligned. What more could I do? What could I change? On a whim, I registered for a dance class at school. I loved learning to break so much that it made sense to me to explore the more traditional side of the art form, something I'd always longed to do more officially.

I fell in love with the studio; I loved the big, tall ceilings, the top-to-bottom windows, and the huge black dance floor before me. Watching the dancers was an emotional experience, too. Their movements were flexible, sensual, uniform in structure, but graceful in execution. I put all my fire and passion into the class, but nothing could make up for the years of formal training some of these students had received. My instructor told me I was naturally gifted, but in many ways, I felt so far behind.

One day, just before class was ready to start, I passed a girl who I had known in high school but we were never really close. There she was, all dressed up in her leotard, with long flowing hair and spine as straight as a sequoia tree.

I stayed behind to watch her piece and was shocked by the sharp realizations that I could see the splinters in her program. Her movements on the surface were fluid, but I could identify the asynchronous motions as she jolted from one place to another, cutting a movement too short and missing the crescendo of the song, not allowing herself to be fully in line with the music. The shock I felt wasn't that she was making mistakes—it was from the bitter taste of regret that surfaced watching her. I felt that it could have been me on stage instead, if only I had taken classes younger; if only I had committed myself sooner.

I could picture myself floating along to the music, extending fully, bounding effortlessly, becoming one with the chords. As much as I loved dancing, it wasn't what I had chosen to pursue. It wasn't the life I had committed to. I knew that even though I had no formal training, that even though I was the one on the sidelines and not on the stage, I had an innate connection to the music and the movements. Seeing her on stage was a reminder of the choices I had made. It was a talisman of regret, an emblem of all the other things I kept saying no to.

My face flushed with the awareness of my own lack of courage, with the pain of having ignored my passion. I had allowed my family to tell me what could make me money, what being responsible meant, and what I should pursue as my life's calling.

I stood alone by the empty stage and assessed myself. I was a Senior in college, just a few credits away from graduating with a major in political science. In many ways, I loved learning societal constructs, trying to create something new, something bold, a new way for us to govern ourselves to make this world a just place.

But I had ignored my passions, and they threatened to rise up and riot inside of me. Every time music plays, even now, the rhythm of my body takes over, the sway of my hips, the grace of my stance, and the stretch of my body. I could feel it all desperately knocking to get out.

I told myself, "No more." I had to move to New York City; I had to model, I had to learn the markets, as well as to make time to dance! I had to follow my dream and express myself completely. What else were we here on this Earth to do than to be ourselves completely?

I got to ArtBar that night full of motivation and flame. And almost immediately, Soul found me. Soul was tall, half-Japanese, and half-white, but he was also full of flavor. I was dating Fever, his best friend, and it was so fun hanging out with them together. I have never laughed so much, from the back and forth banter, the ways they would "gig" on each other. It was an endless burning and laughing session.

"Yo, you and Jojo are killing it on the dance floor these days. Fever and I were chillin', and I came up with something," he said.

"What is it?" I asked, proud and flattered.

"We were talking about *Invasion of the Body Snatchers*! Yo, then I was like, 'Invasion of the B-GIRLS!!' He smiled his million-watt smile and continued. "Here's the idea: an all-girls hip-hop event, it would be so dope! You could have all the girls—writers, emcees, and deejays—the first ever in Seattle. You'd have to have all the hip-hop elements represented, but it would be so fresh. What do you think?"

"Yes!" I screamed. I had never agreed to anything so quickly in my life. "That is so, so dope! Jojo and I could really make it so phenomenal; I know we could."

Whatever I had been searching for, whatever outlet I needed, I could feel in my bones that this was it. I was hyped up. I called Jojo, who was one of my best friends in the scene, the second I got home and pitched her the idea. She was in! We started masterminding right away about talking to different emcees.

I called Honey, and Jojo called Asia-One, but they were already booked. We called Anomalies, but we couldn't afford the whole crew. I was so sad because I wanted BigTara there, too. We were able to get Kuttin' Kandi, and Ndidi was in for sure!

We talked a lot about the vision, the space, the fashion, and the emcees, with Tre in charge of marketing. Jojo managed sponsorships, and I planned the logistics for the venue, like nailing down the URL and calling the artists. We also got all these urban clothing lines to contribute to the fashion show. We would get all the b-boys as our models. Dedos from Canada did the flyer.

Jojo and I planned tirelessly for weeks to get all the details in order. The whole crew was behind us, and the word on the street was that this event was going to be huge. The days ticked by as all the pieces fell into place. We were getting the players in order, all the details sorted.

We scheduled Friday night for the main event and Saturday for the younger crowd. Unfortunately, I already knew I had to miss the Saturday event, but it was for a good reason. I was flying out early Saturday morning for my brother Paul's 30th birthday party. He had rented out a whole restaurant in Manhattan to celebrate, and I couldn't miss it.

Before we knew it, the day was here. The place was packed with people; the energy was high, the vibe was intense. Looking around, I couldn't believe we had pulled it off. To think, in mere minutes, we'd get to see all our planning and hard work turned into action.

Just then, a voice cut through the noise—we were off!

"B- b- b-girls and b- b- b-boys!!!!! All around the world!!!!" The music blared and sounded so tight, with the fashion show up first. Our models—Hews, Soul, Fever, Sneke, DVone—looked so fly. We had all the smooth brothers modeling, and Unika from Brand Nubian Designs brought the female models.

When the fashion show was over, the ladies of rhyme started spitting—Kylea! Yamuna on skates! Followed by powerful performances from Spyce-E, Ndidi Cascade from Vancouver, BC, Solstice, EBteck, T.H.C., PaigeOne, and Peace—it was just an outstanding lineup.

Of course, as organizers and breakers on the crew, Jojo and I performed, too. Fever choreographed our routine for the event, and even though we were nervous, we had practiced, practiced, and practiced even more. We had a few songs lined up for our piece and were ready to go, but then out into the cipher stumbled a very drunk, very high brother to mess us up.

I'm sure that he had no idea that the brown-skinned b-girls right in front of him had produced the show, but we'd try to start our dance, and then he'd come out again into the cipher to disrupt our flow. Finally, someone hauled him out, which helped keep our agenda on track. I was so looking forward to stepping away from managing the logistics to take the time to rock out.

We did our very best that night, giving all of ourselves to life, to our dreams, and to hip hop. It was one of the proudest moments of my life, and it simply blew away all of our expectations. I looked out onto the crowd and saw so many people there to celebrate this culture we loved, all these bodies moving together to the beat, and my heart was full. We had made this, all this happiness, all these memories, out of Soul's idea. I had set my mind to it, and it had played out even better than I could have hoped.

But I had to leave it. I ran into Jojo and told her, "Girl, I have to catch my flight early tomorrow morning!" We hugged and congratulated each other, and the next morning, with little sleep in me, I boarded the plane to New York City and felt like I was the one who had wings. I arrived and rested at Paul's place, then stepped out of my brother's building and into the crowds of people rippling up and down Carmine Street. I could actually wear a skirt and an elegant top with no sleeves. The weather was warm, and the city felt alive.

Most of my family was there: Carol, Johanna, my mom, Shirley, and my dad, too. When we got to the restaurant, we didn't know many people—most of them were Paul's friends from work or school—but we're Quinteros, and we love to socialize! The music started, and we danced the whole night. Salsa, after salsa, Celia Cruz, Willie Colon, Johnny Pacheco, merengue, Elvis, Proyecto Uno, some true R&B, and the owners even let us stay longer because they had such a blast, too! Hours later, I had to get some water and catch my breath, so I stepped out onto the sidewalk.

I leaned up against the awning, looked down the street, and a strange feeling washed over me. It felt like I was vibrating, like I was fully present like I was truly myself. I couldn't remember ever feeling so alive as I did at that moment, and this was *after* my crew's ArtBar performance. I could have screamed, so deep was the relief that I didn't have to dim my light to make others feel comfortable, that I didn't have to make myself feel small to fit in. Even with everything going great in my life, there was something undeniable about New York City, something that amplified it.

The next day, tired but still energetic, we walked down to Wall Street to see the action, and as I looked up, I saw two familiar figures cutting through the blue of the sky: the Twin Towers. We took the elevator to the top floor, so high above the city, so high above the Earth that you could see its curve. I looked out, wondering if I could somehow see the bend of my own life before me, the trajectory of my own path. We snapped a picture together as a family; I always wanted to remember the happiness I felt in that moment, the love and hope and promise of it all.

I came back home with such a renewed spirit, only to be reminded of what I was coming back to. Seattle felt like such a small town after the bright lights of Manhattan, so dreary, disrupted only by my increasingly passive-aggressive work environment that was churning rapidly over to just aggressive-aggressive.

My first Monday back at work felt interminable, the monotony broken up by a phone call from a familiar number: my mother.

"*Tengo buen noticias!*" *I have good news.* The universe must have known I could use some.

"Tell me? What's going on?"

"*La Cira se va casar con Marcos!*" *Cira is going to marry Marcos.*

"Ohhhhhh!" I squealed. I was so happy that our Tia Cira, my mom's dear old friend for years and one of my Colombian aunts, had found such happiness. All our Colombian Tias lived in Bellevue and have been in our lives since I was five years old.

"*So, mami, cuando es la boda?*" I asked my mom. *So, mom, when is the wedding?*

"*Abril,*" she responded. "*Voy a Seattle tenemos que ir con Carol y Bryan.*" *April. I'll come to Seattle, and we'll go with Carol and Bryan*, my sister and nephew.

I was so thrilled to have that to look forward to. I got off the phone brimming with this bright news and optimistically checked in with the basic task of printing out a bunch of labels for the program filing system that I had given the office assistant, Karen. She was my angry boss's right hand and split her time between our department and another, so she never seemed to have time for the tasks I gave her. She also seemingly had no interest in learning or growing, and this was my first management role, so all I could do was show her the steps.

"Karen, how are the labels coming?"

But instead of giving an answer, she seethed with unrestrained anger. I had already spoken to HR about the situation, but nothing really happened—they just told me to hold off on using email and to have a meeting with the director, my boss. I was just trying to do my best with the situation I was in, which was an increasingly difficult task with each passing day.

"Karen, can you answer me, please?"

"Why don't you just do the labels yourself if you want them so badly."

"Because you are the office assistant for the department, and I have to meet with the teachers and need administrative help."

"Well, it's not in my wheelhouse. I think you should just add it to your daily tasks," she said, smacking gum with her feet up on the desk.

I was patient, probably too patient, and asked her to come with me to the printer so I could show her the steps. As I entered the printer room and said hello to a passing colleague, Karen, who was behind me, stuck out her foot and tripped me. I barely caught myself, and all I could hear was the sound of her caustic laughter.

"Oh, you better watch yourself," she chuckled.

I was red in the face with anger. "Don't trip me!" I said.

"Oh, what are you going to do? Cry about it?"

I was so frustrated that I marched straight to the Dean's office. I told him everything that was happening, and to his credit, he listened, though he blamed himself. He ran through his reasons, but each one felt flimsy when held against the day-to-day that I had endured for so many months.

"No more," I said once he had finished. "It's either her or me."

And at that point, my gut told me that even if she *did* leave, I didn't know how much longer I could stay. Is this what success looks like? Become a college graduate, get your own office, land that lonely sought-after leadership position, live at home, and just dream of the day you do what you really want to do, which in my case, was dance, model, and live in the Big Apple?

Up to this point, I'd had many chances to live, but I had so many fears and so many missed opportunities. I felt stuck. I felt desperate. I felt so close to what I knew was my path but so far from being able to get it.

In a few short weeks, it was time to go to the wedding. As I got ready in my room, staring longingly at the posters and photos on my wall, my collection of memory and dreams, I couldn't help but think more about those missed opportunities and what I was longing for. In the short run, at least, I was looking forward to seeing my family and to having some fun together.

Fever and I had taken a break—though we were still connected, he had moved to New York to pursue his dreams. We all knew there wasn't a better city for breaking than NYC. I was proud of him. His choice stuck with me—an inspiration from afar.

Months had gone by after he left, and I started dating a youth counselor I met while out on the town. I got him a gift, a beautiful gray suit so he could look professional for all the youths he supported in court, and even though we hadn't known each other too long, I had never seen the look on his face when he opened the bag.

"This is my first suit," he said.

"This will be the first of many," I replied. "You know, I have a great place you could break it in. A dear family friend is getting married in a few weeks, and I'd like you to come with me."

He hesitated. "You know I don't really like group settings, but I'll think about it."

"It'll be fun," I said. "Keep me posted—I'd love for you to come."

The morning of the wedding, my mom and Carol picked me up, and I called him to see if he could make it, but there was no answer. I left the address on his voicemail.

It wasn't a far drive, and we arrived in time to see my gorgeous Tia Cira, the bride, put on her makeup. A statuesque, beautiful, and brilliant woman, Cira was someone you couldn't help but look up to, a dentist from Columbia who was both gorgeous and a hard worker devoted to her family.

The wedding was beautiful. Afterward, the toasts began, the music started playing, and I hadn't had a drink in over a year, so the champagne was extra amazing! Carol and I were dancing and drinking, but what kept my heart aching was looking over at our table and seeing the seat next to me empty. I was already feeling alone, but to not have him there, just made me so sad. I would look at all the couples on the dance floor and feel so upset that I started to cry. I didn't want to ruin the celebration with my tears, so I decided to call him in the hopes it might make me feel better to hear his voice. I left the restaurant where we were having the reception and spotted a payphone next door. I put in my quarters, and after a few rings, he answered.

"Hi, hon, how are you doing? Did you have to work today?"

"Nope, not today."

"What are you up to, then?"

"Not much," he said, his voice flat. "I'm just playing video games."

I could hear the sounds of synthesized gunfire in the background.

"Why didn't you call me then?"

"I was just relaxing, babe."

"But you knew how much I was looking forward to you coming with me to this wedding."

He was quiet on the line. In the background, from his video game, I heard an explosion.

And I lost it. I didn't have my own place; I was being attacked and undervalued at work, and I wasn't living my dream, I was across the country from the one place I wanted to call home and the one person who made me feel so loved. Every part of me felt trapped. Every part of me felt like I was going to explode.

"How could you?" I yelled. "How could you do this to me?"

I didn't know if I was yelling at him or myself.

My sister came running outside.

"Annabel, why are you yelling? The whole reception can hear you!"

All I could do was cry.

"Stay here," she said. "I'll go get Bryan and mom, and we can go. We'll talk in the car."

Bryan came out and hugged me. Mom followed.

"*Que te pasa?*" she yelled. "*No puedo creer como te fuiste, y estabas llorando y gritando!*" *I can't believe how you left, and you were crying and screaming!*

"Mom, Annabel doesn't need to hear this right now, please just get in the car," Carol said.

We all piled into the car and started driving home, but my mom didn't hold back.

"*Ni tengo palabras, no puedo creer que te portaste asi, en fuente de todos, en la boda. Que te pasa!? Que van a pensar la gente!?*" *I have no words. I cannot believe that you behaved like this, in everyone's name, at the wedding. What's wrong!? What are people going to think!?*

I was consumed with the pain of doing everything right but having nothing go right, of not being valued by the person I was with, of not feeding my soul by living my dreams.

I couldn't hold it in.

"I!" I yelled, my fist slamming upward into the windshield.

"Don't!" I punched the glass again.

"Care!" The windshield splintered into a fractured web.

"What!" Punch.

"People!" My knuckles of steel.

"Think!" The pain was a release, interrupted by my family's screams. And then there was silence. I remember hearing in my Wing Chun class about how to exert beyond your target, and I definitely did it because I didn't even feel it. I lightly broke my skin, but my bones were fine.

Bryan's sweet voice broke the silence, "Tia, it's okay, I know you're angry, but it's okay. We all get angry sometimes."

And then all the tears came gushing out like a waterfall. Because he was right, I was just as he said. So angry. So sad. And so alone. I had done everything I was supposed to do to make my family proud and build a cookie-cutter life. But I was consumed by frustration and fury.

Carol pulled the car over, and I felt my mother's hand on my shoulder. I felt comfort but also confident that this was it for me. I wasn't going to seek anyone's approval anymore. I decided then and there that the life I had been living was over—the end.

But it was also a beginning. There was only one path for me now.

I was moving to New York City.

2

In All My Wildest Dreams

t was a sticky summer, the kind of heat that presses down on you from above. But I felt light as air. It was August, and I was moving to New York.

Claire, with whom I had roomed in college, was coming with me. We packed our bags and put all we needed in her small sedan, ready to hit the road.

With my life savings in my pocket and fueled by the fire of my big city dream, we drove east on I-90. We weren't taking the scenic route— no sleep till Brooklyn.

On our way out of Washington State, we passed Snoqualmie, Ellensburg, and memories of Girls State flashed through my mind. Then Walla Walla, where College Place was, one of the Seventh-Day Adventist universities my dad attended.

We pushed east through Idaho, through the forests and mountains of green. It reminded us both of camping when we were younger, all of us kids of color packed into a big white truck commissioned by the church. We remembered coasting through the wilderness before Habb's clutch went out, and we had to pull over. When the van stopped, Habb, a darker-skinned brother, looked up. The van had stopped right in front of a big sign reading "Aryan Nation."

It wasn't the first time we had seen anything that blatantly racist, but there was protection in the city, the baked-in accountability of having thousands of other people around. Out here, civilization seemed a lot less civilized. It was the first time that we realized how close we lived to it.

Habb fixed the car, and when he got back in, we could see his whole body trembling from fear.

"I really thought I was going to get lynched," he said, voice and hands shaking. At first, I thought he was crying, but then laughter poured out of him, a mix of relief and disbelief.

Spurred on by the memory and the fact that New York was seemingly on the horizon, we sped through the rest of Idaho and burst into Montana. We didn't stop unless we had to, pausing just once for a short nap on the side of the road. We looped through Illinois, got stuck in Chicago traffic, and kept moving on. Once we got into Ohio, the road ahead was clear. I really couldn't believe we were seeing purple mountains; I thought that was just a verse in our anthem.

My brother lived in the West Village, on Carmine Street. When we got there, we were exhausted and learned our first NYC lesson: there was nowhere to park! We found a spot that felt like it was miles away, but when we knocked on Paul's apartment door, the trek was worth it. He was so happy to see us and wasted no time showing us around and laying down some ground rules to keep us safe and savvy.

We walked to Washington Square Park, which was filled with music, people playing chess, roller skaters, Rastafarians, brothers selling ready-to-smoke blunts, and students and professionals scattered about. Claire and I were taking in the sun, the sounds, and the people and couldn't believe that just two days ago we were in Seattle.

Soon it was time for Claire to leave. We had planned to spend the summer together, but New York had worked its magic on her quickly. She had realized a dream of her own—there was a man in her life who she loved, and he deserved to be told. We said goodbye to her, and then it was just Paul and me in his little matchbox apartment.

Those first two weeks were all about living out loud, exploring the nightlife, eating the best food I could get my hands on, staying up until dawn, and dancing until my muscles ached. One time while out with my brother at a crowded restaurant with a friendly vibe, a man caught my eye, and I caught his. We smiled and said hello, and a small thrill ran through me.

I continued to the bar, and while waiting for a drink, he came up alongside. The conversation flowed easily between us, small talk that seemed like a promise of more to come.

"I'm Julius," he said. "I'd love to talk more. Here's my card. Call me so we can go out for dinner."

"That sounds lovely," I replied because it truly did.

Julius left after that, and my brother swooped in.

"Who was that?" he asked.

"We just met. He's an attorney for Lehman Brothers."

The rest of the night was spent laughing and talking with my brother and his city friends. It was all quite magical, actually being here, actually being a part of the place I'd so long dreamed of. But as fun as it was to stay with Paul, it wasn't the full life I had come all this way for.

I turned Julius' business card around in my hand and made a promise to myself: I would get a job, make some money, and find a place of my own.

I signed up with a temp agency that had a good record of placing people in long-term assignments. My first job was working in the production department of Marcellus, a marketing company on Park Avenue.

There were perks to the job—they saw potential in me, music played throughout the office, and it was in a great location. In my first week, I heard familiar lyrics pump through the speakers and ran to the manager.

"Excuse me," I said, a bit breathless. "Who sings this song?"

"It's Bocelli, I think," he replied. He didn't know it, but he had just solved a mystery I'd tried to find an answer to for years. I had heard the song in my dreams and always wondered how that was possible, why my subconscious had latched onto it so strongly, but I could never figure out who sang it. After a few years, I had stopped looking.

And now, at my first job in the city of my dreams, here it was again.

"Do you know what it's called?" I asked him.

"'Time to Say Goodbye,'" he replied.

Goodbye, Seattle. Hello to my future.

With a steady gig going, I turned my energy to searching for an apartment, which could be a full-time job in NYC. I looked all around Brooklyn and in the Bronx. I fell in love with a place in Park Slope but knew it was a neighborhood with rapidly rising rents. I knew I didn't want roommates, which meant that finding something affordable was even more of a challenge.

Really, I wanted to be close to Fever and his roommate Lil Lep, who lived in the Bronx, in the Kingsbridge neighborhood, my only two friends in New York. Lep was a legendary b-boy, the pioneer of the head spin, a move in which the breaker's entire body balanced vertically on the crown of their head; he was one of the best at it in the world. I remember seeing him, it was the first b-boy crew performance for a presidential inauguration, President Regan's, to be exact, on TV in my living room, where I watched it as a starry-eyed kid. Now I literally lived blocks away from Lil Lep, one of the stars of that performance, a true hip-hop architect who was now a dear friend. He would bring so much passion to the moment with his creative presence, but he was also one of the kindest, most genuine and giving people I had ever met.

I found a place on Grand Concourse that checked all the boxes—it was in a central location, it felt homey and funky with arched hallways and small details, and it was easy to get to and from. I put down a deposit, but they were renovating it, and it was going to be weeks before I could move in.

Weeks turned into a month, and I got more and more frustrated with not being able to truly be on my own. I approached the property manager and asked for my deposit back, but I got no return phone calls or mail, so I went to their office, and they refused to return it to me. I'm sure they expected me, a young girl new to city life, to just roll over and accept it. But they didn't know who they were dealing with.

I filed a small claims court injunction, and one week later, I got a call from the property manager letting me know they had my money. When I arrived, they chastised me for taking that course of action.

"You didn't have to take us to court," she said sheepishly.

"Actually, I did," I replied, looking her square in the eyes. "The laws exist to protect people like me from people like you."

I walked out triumphant, breathing in the early-fall air, feeling the power in my veins, the confidence in me building day by day. Next step: new apartment. No matter what.

A few days later, I saw a one-bedroom, one block off the 1 line. It was on 231st Street in Kingsbridge, and I loved everything about it—the French doors, the tree outside the window, the feeling of seclusion and safety. Fever and Lil Lep came by to check it out, and they were impressed.

"But you might not get it, Annabel," said Lep.

I asked why, and he replied, "This is known as a white-only block. Look at all the names in the foyer. They're all Mcs or Macs or 'inskys.'"

But soon, there was a Quintero—I moved in at the end of October. Fever helped me with all my stuff, the two of us carrying boxes by hand and carts onto the train. We tried to get on at West 4th Street but ran smack into the biggest Halloween parade I had ever seen in my life! It was like a carnival. We were just trying to maneuver our way onto the train, passing people dressed like Britney Spears and Ronald McDonald partying left and right, singing and dancing with bottles in hand. I had never seen anything like it—tens of thousands of people, massive energy, celebration on an epic scale.

When we got to my apartment and opened the door, I was greeted with the best sound I had ever heard—total silence. It was all my own, every corner and every cubby. That night, I slept soundly on a mattress on the floor, all by myself for the first time in my life.

I was in a groove, and things were falling into place. Next on my list: secure my first photo shoot, my first catwalk, my first anything as a model. I submitted my 8x10 and bio at Empire, a modeling and artist agency in 42nd Street.

A few weeks later, I was hanging with b-boy crew Hierophysics—Fever, Fabel, Ness, Jazzy Jay, and Sweepey—and we took the train to Grand Central Station to head down to CBGB's Gallery for a performance. It was a Friday night, and we decided to walk a little bit since we had been on the train for a while.

We walked down 3rd, and the fellas were in fine form, giggin' on clothes, what was happening with politics and culture, then just people. I got a call that flashed the word "Empire" on my phone's screen, but I didn't want to pick up because it was so loud. When we got to CBGB's, Christy Z was already there. She had worked with the managers of the spot to coordinate the show.

I was sitting with Christy Z while the fellas got ready when Fever came up to me.

"Hey, we're about to go up, and you know what? You should come and get down. I know the crowd would love to see a b-girl."

I turned bright red and suppressed the urge to preemptively say no out of embarrassment. Instead, I breathed in, exhaling slowly.

"I'd love to," I said.

I walked through the packed crowd and up to the stage. Together, I stood with the crew behind the curtain. Fabel and Jazzy were talking about how to warm up the crowd, and they both turned their heads to me.

"Annabel, you should go out first, right in between Ness and Fever. Show them what a b-girl can do."

Ness and Fever dashed out, and when it was my cue, I joined them. I top rocked, got down, and did my footwork, and it got a little slippery because the floor had wax on it, but I more than held my own. It was so dope! To dance with Pop Master Fabel, who I had watched for years, and Jazzy Jay—it was like a dream.

Fever came off stage. "That floor was mad slippery!" He must have seen the worried look on my face. "But they didn't notice. All they saw was that you were feeling it with tons of energy. You rocked it."

I had never smiled that big in my life. I sat down with Christy.

"You were great, girl. I love to see you dance!" she exclaimed. "And now you can say you've danced at CBGB's Gallery, an iconic NYC spot.

It was everything. To be with these legends, to dance, to be on my way to living my dreams.

The next day, I checked my messages and called Empire back.

The agent who answered didn't mince any words. "If I call you, you have to answer immediately. Jay-Z wanted you for his next video, but I couldn't reach you, so I had to give it to another girl."

My heart sank. Jay-Z! I had been that close to something so big. Why hadn't I picked up the call? But then I realized: I had traded one big dream for another. Other chances would come. This was just the beginning for me, I could feel it, and nothing could bring me down.

A few weeks later, I got a call from the staffing agency: a boutique hedge fund was looking for an office manager and administrative assistant, someone who could handle their processes and paperwork. I had been working as a temp at Deutsche Bank in the famous Lipstick Building, but the office politics were too much, and the work was too routine, so I jumped at the new opportunity.

I took a cab downtown, the first time I had taken one since arriving in New York. I loved it. Being in a car makes you see the city in a whole other light. I put the window down and let the cool breeze wash over me. I could feel fall in the air.

The cabbie pulled up to my destination: World Trade Center, Tower 1. Looking up at all those stories of glass and steel, I flashed back to the last time I had been here for my brother Paul's 30th birthday right after the Invasion of the B-Girls, almost exactly one year earlier. Back then, I couldn't wait to make this town my home, and a year later, I had made it. I lived here, and soon, with any luck, I would work here.

I entered the lobby and met a tall Taiwanese young professional. "Hi, Annabel, I'm George," he said. I soon learned that George and his father had together started the firm and brought with them more than their fair share of market brilliance.

We went up in the elevator 42 stories, and my ears popped with the swift change in altitude. When the elevator stopped, we walked into a small little office with a few scattered cubicles.

"We're still getting set up," said George, gesturing to the sparse space. "That's where you come in."

His father joined us, and it was more of a conversation than an interview. In the end, we shook hands, and I left convinced this would be the perfect job for me. But there was one thing holding me back.

When I left the building, I called Christy Z. "Girl, I just had the best interview. I know I'd learn so much, but there's a problem: it's in the World Trade Center."

"Why is that a problem?" she asked.

"It's a little scary. Remember when people tried to blow it up in '93? What if it happens again?"

Christy, who was a Muslim, laid down some truth.

"No terrorist represents our faith, and those men committed a terrible sin. You shouldn't let something from the past influence your decision. Did you like the people you met?"

"Absolutely. They seemed like a really nice family."

"Then don't let what happened years ago dictate your future."

The next day, I got a call from the headhunter, and I picked it up on the first ring.

"They want to move forward and offer you the job."

I was thrilled, and after negotiating a few finer points, accepted the offer.

I started on Monday; it took an hour to get there from the Bronx. I was a commuter now, standing the whole ride on the express train, being a part of the massive crowd that pushed up the subway stairs and into the mall.

The first day was spent getting me through the proper clearance applications and making sure I passed background checks. After a long day of being verified and vetted, I was ready to head home to start in earnest the following day. On my way back to the subway station, I passed a magazine stand and saw something that made my heart skip a beat: the February issue of *Blaze*, a hip-hop magazine.

Months earlier, Fabel, a legendary pop master, approached Fever and the crew to see if we wanted to be included in a spread of b-boys and b-girls for an upcoming edition. We went to the shoot decked to the nines and struck some poses for the photographer. Having wanted to model my entire life, it was exhilarating getting to be on set. Ultimately, we didn't know if we'd be included or not—they made it clear there were no guarantees—but I was anxious to see who made it in. Would this be my first time in print? Would I see my friends? I bought a few copies and hurried over to my platform.

When I got on the train, I was burning up inside, so anxious to see what could be, but we were packed into the car so tightly, there was no room to even raise my arms. Finally, once people got off on 96th Street, my arms were free.

I pulled one out carefully, not wanting to crease it, and cracked it open to the table of contents. A quick scan showed a picture of Will Smith … and me! Right next to him!

I smiled so big I could have lit up the city. I was in a *magazine*. I was officially a *model*.

I couldn't believe I had only officially been living in NYC for six months, and my life had changed so much. I was happy in a way I didn't know was possible. I had gotten this life because I had *chosen* this life.

I got off at my stop at 231st Street, and the air had never smelled better, the grit of the city never so beautiful, the light never as vibrant as right then and there. From a bodega came the sound of one of my favorite songs—Whitney Houston's "One Moment in Time"—and I sang along out loud for all to hear.

I want one moment in time when I'm more than I thought I could be. When all of my dreams are a heartbeat away, and the answers are all up to me. Give me one moment in time when I'm racing with destiny. In that one moment of time, I will feel, I will feel eternity.

And it didn't stop there. I dug into my new job with passion and purpose, so eager to learn the way things worked, to pick the brains of these two powerhouse businessmen, to learn the markets and the way money works on a worldwide scale.

It was a crash course. A lot of it was managing hedge-fund paperwork to ensure FCC compliance, but I also learned how to trade, how to read the right kind of news, which companies to watch, what the tickers meant, the different platforms, and which industries they housed.

I had never learned so much so quickly. I would get in by 8 a.m. and leave at 8 p.m. In the morning, I'd study the markets during the day, take care of client documents and investment paperwork, and at night, although I was exhausted, get caught up with the Asian markets to be read for the 9:30 a.m. bell.

Mr. Lin, Sr., was one of the sharpest people I had ever met, and his son had certainly inherited his dad's impressive intellect. They worked so well as a team, digging deep into a company's psyche, an industry's history, a competitor's strategy. They batted information back and forth like elite athletes on a field, leaving no angle unturned, no approach unconsidered. And it paid off because the company was growing at lightning speed.

In many ways, I felt right at home. I could take in massive amounts of information and make sense of them. My synapses were firing on all cylinders, and the Lins were impressed with my ability to keep up. But in other ways, I was still a sheltered girl who hadn't grown up around this level of money.

One day, one of our clients wanted to invest in a different class of funds, and I was asked to do a wire transfer. As I found the file and updated the bank details, Mr. Lin, Sr., handed me a note with the amount of the transfer.

My face flushed. I had never seen so many zeroes: $1,000,000.00.

I grabbed the note with two hands as though it was breakable, as though the paper it was written on was worth as much as the printed numbers. I knew transfers had to be done in time for the account to be reconciled, but I couldn't stop checking the routing information, the date, and the littlest details.

When I felt confident enough to press print, I realized my cheeks were red, and my temperature was high, so I got up to get the printout and took a moment to breathe deep before bringing it to George to double-check before pressing send.

George smiled. "It looks great, Annabel!"

I brought it to Mr. Lin, Sr., who looked at it closely. He lifted his chin, and his golden framed glasses slid to the tip of his nose.

"Looks great, Annabel," he said just like his son, but this time there was pride laced through the words.

I typed each number, and each button had its own weight. I realized how much they trusted me. I realized how much the clients trusted them.

The machine locked in the paper, and as it slowly scanned, my heart fluttered. I was watching everything, hoping the paper wouldn't jam, listening intently to the different sounds and ways the fax was going through and then hearing that jingle. It went through, and I waited for confirmation. Nothing was complete until there was proof.

"Mr. Lin, I have the confirmation here and the original wiring request."

"Thank you, Annabel. I appreciate that you gave this your full attention. That is how we differentiate ourselves from the rest of the field. We focus, and we follow through. Showing how much you value your client is best done through consistency and persistence. Trust and our word are all we have, so we must be impeccable with both." He smiled, and I smiled.

"Were you nervous?" he asked, just as I was turning to leave.

"Petrified," I replied.

"Just wait until it's an even bigger number."

"How much bigger?"

He shrugged. "$1,000,000.00 is the minimum."

I took the train home that night, eager to get back to the Bronx. The crew was coming to my place that night, a rare occasion, and were waiting for me there.

"Turn on the music," I said after we got into the apartment. "I need to change and get settled."

When I came back to the living room, everyone laughed.

"What?" I asked

"You come in here with your Wall Street suit on and then come out with a b-girl stance!" said Alien Ness, another member of the crew, through his laughter. I couldn't help but join in—the duality of my life was real.

"That's my life right now," I said. "Rockin' it on Wall Street and back here in the Boogie Down!"

We played music and danced that whole night. I loved the contrast, the two halves of the life I built. The financial and the fun, the downtown and the uptown.

The following week, I was getting lunch at Menchanko-Tei and heard my name.

"Hello, Annabel."

I turned quickly—no one knew me downtown. To my surprise, it was Julius, the man I had met when I first moved here. I had never called him; I was just busy getting my life together, seeing where the city might take me. We caught up and made small talk, and even though it had been months, there was still a spark between us.

"You like sushi?" he asked.

"I love it."

"Then let's go out for sushi some time," he replied, a sparkle in his eye. "Here's my card again. Don't lose it this time."

I laughed. It sounded like a challenge. I ran my finger along the edge of his card and said, "I'll call you," with all the sassiness I could muster. I left and could feel him watch me as I walked back to work.

I kept my word, and a few weeks later, Julius and I were meeting in the lobby of World Trade Center, Tower 2, to finally have our first date.

When I arrived, security asked, "Windows of the World"?

Julius nodded. "We have a reservation."

The doors opened, and as the music washed over us, the view was unparalleled. Located on the 84th floor, it was the highest restaurant in the world. On the dance floor, couples were expertly twirling, dipping, and moving together with the city twinkling behind them.

Julius and I got a seat at the bar and ordered sushi with shrimp tempura. It was so fresh and savory, and we ordered several rounds of martinis to wash it all down. I liked him. And looking around at the endless lights of Manhattan, I truly loved my life for the first time.

As the days and weeks went by, my life fell into a pattern: I loved my job, I had my people. Some of us went out a few days later, but when I got home, I couldn't fall asleep, but when my alarm buzzed to life in the morning, beckoning me to wake by playing Joe Sample's "In All My Wildest Dreams," my eyes were too heavy to open. When I finally did, I realized it was past 7 a.m., and my bed had never felt so comfortable. I hadn't taken a sick day yet, so it felt like the perfect opportunity to sleep in and enjoy a promising September day.

But I couldn't. There were only three of us in the office, and the work would not wait, so I jumped out of bed and started getting dressed. I walked through my living room to the bathroom, tugging clothes on, frantically forming my hair into a bun. Just outside, I heard the loud sound of a crow calling out.

After brushing my teeth, I rushed to my bedroom window. I had a maple tree on the other side of it, but the summer songbirds I was used to hearing each morning had never sounded as crisp and clear as the caw of the black-winged bird.

Stepping up to the glass, I realized it wasn't just one bird—it was a treeful.

"What is happening?" I asked them. "What are you trying to tell me?"

They chattered in return, and for a few moments, I was lost in the conversation. I had heard whispers as a child of what they meant: they were shapeshifters, change bringers. What change would this day bring for me?

But I was late, so late, and snapped out of it in time to get the essentials together. Knowing I'd have to run to catch the train, I opted for Easy Spirit snakeskin ankle boots instead of my usual heels, preferring speed over style. I rocketed out my door, booked it the few blocks to the train platform, and made it onto the subway just as the door closed.

While my train headed south on Broadway, I had a smile on my face all the way to work. I got off at my stop, went to Cornucopia to get my favorite oat and raisin natural energy bar, and of course, picked up today's *Financial Times* and *Wall Street Journal*. I thanked the guys at the shop and hurried to work. Looking up at the two giant structures, I felt a surge of pride—how lucky was I that this is where I get to come to every day?

I passed through security, fended off the jocular advances from one of my favorite maintenance workers, and took the elevator up to the 46th floor. Everyone greeted each other with a half-smile and "have a good day." Walking into the office at 8:40 a.m., I noticed Mr. Lin's sweater on the back of his chair and cringed—I hated being late. But he was nowhere to be seen, so perhaps there was still hope my morning mishap wouldn't be discovered.

I settled into my desk, nestled in a half-cubicle, and opened up the paper to learn what was happening. Skimming over the news of the day, struck by the inequity in the markets and in the world, I was plagued by a familiar thought—what if multinational companies were required to pay a global minimum wage? Instead of capitalizing on the fiscal loopholes and lack of global oversight that ultimately punish the workers in the countries in which these organizations operate, a global minimum wage would go a long way in stabilizing the—

...

The Earth shook from above my head.

3

The September Fall

t was an earthquake; I was sure of it. The building swayed. The doorways tilted. The walls shook. But somehow, instead of being underfoot, the rumbling was skyward, overhead and seemingly all around. I ran to the window of Mr. Lin's office, half-expecting to see buildings bent and crumbling all around, but the city looked just like it always did, gleaming in the mid-September sunlight.

A bomb, then, I thought. A fleet of cannons. An explosion of some sort—a gas line flickering then bursting into flame. Or something otherworldly, an unnatural weight that fell on top of this tower.

Standing in Mr. Lin's office, I glanced down at his desk, and he smiled back at me from a picture of him and his wife with a rainbow stretching out behind them in Vancouver, Washington. They were younger then, relaxed, confident, at peace. I reached out for the frame—*where was he?*—but before I could grab it, the floor tilted away from me, the picture falling to the ground.

Whatever was causing this, it wasn't stopping. I needed to move, to talk to someone, to try to figure out what was happening. Sprinting to my cubicle, I grabbed my purse and sweater and ran to the front of the office, wrenching open the front door. Just as I did, an Asian man I'd never met before burst out of the space to the right of ours. We stood rigid in our respective doorways, stunned. I had so many questions, but seeing my own fear reflected back at me in the face of a stranger left me momentarily voiceless.

The building shook again, and I stumbled as the door swung on its hinges toward me, almost knocking me down. I braced myself, digging in my toes and clutching the doorframe to stay upright. The floor seemed to ripple underfoot.

I looked up, and the stranger adjacent to me was unblinking. The building shifted, and our doors began a long swing, left to right, taking us with them. I braced myself, held out my arm, flinging my full weight against mine to stop its arc. As I did, he jumped back into his office, flying backward, and the door slammed hard and fast, the sound like a clap of thunder.

I glanced back into my own office. Growing up, earthquake drills in the Seattle public school system had taught me to duck and cover, to crawl underneath a table or desk for protection. But here on the 46th floor, my desk had boxes and boxes of records and files underneath. My instinct was to take shelter there, but there was no place for me.

I closed my eyes.

"*Ahh Dios mio, que hago!*" I thought. "*Oh my God, what should I do?*"

I opened them, and the lush, lively office filled with vibrant colors and polished wood had somehow transformed. All the brightness had faded, and where I had been sitting was suddenly washed with tones of muted gray. No ash had fallen. No smoke had yet filled the air. To me, it was a clear message: *this is no place for the living. It is time to leave, Annabel.*

The tower seemed to groan, twisting and swaying, shifting the world all around me. I was confused. I was terrified and unprepared. But I listened to the voice inside of me that spoke.

I said out loud, "Okay, Annabel. You have to try. Try to get out of the building, even if you have to die trying."

And then I ran.

The floor was a jagged landscape, uneven and unpredictable. The building rolled, throwing me left and right. Each unforgiving step forward was a Herculean effort, my feet falling too far or catching the ground too quickly. My knees buckled, my arms knocking into walls that shouldn't have been so close and grasping emptily for those that should have been near but were perpetually out of reach.

The shaking was relentless, bouncing me left and right as I tried and failed to stay balanced. I was being thrown around like a ragdoll in a funhouse as I pushed forward and prayed to God to please keep the building whole. The floor arched and bowed. The ceiling was an undulating ocean of beams and plaster above me. Onward was my only goal, and it was getting more difficult by the minute.

And then, just as quickly as it had started, it stopped. The building settled as 1,368 feet of steel and souls found their footing again. I wasted no seconds and sprinted toward the stairway door, breathing out my relief as I ran before panic, acrid and sharp, took its place. Why weren't the alarms ringing? Why weren't there announcements, instructions on how to stay calm, where to go, reminding us to be safe? Where were the other people on this floor? What if I was somehow the only one still alive?

I found myself standing and staring at the stairway door, remembering fire drills from Stevenson Elementary. Touch the doorknob with a single finger, they taught us. If it feels hot, do not open it! Run to another door. Use a window. Find another way.

I reached out, resting a finger on the metal. My fear was overwhelming, overpowering my senses. I wrapped my whole hand around the doorknob, closing my eyes, willing myself to feel something definitive. Still, nothing came to me. *Be patient*, I told myself, fighting the fear that surged through my skin. It took every inch of me, but I was able to block everything else out in order to create a small space to listen to the story my synapses could tell, so thankful for the meditation I'd done in the past. *Hot or cold?* I asked. I breathed. *Hot or cold?*

Cold was the answer.

I twisted the handle and opened the door, slowly at first, preparing myself for more horror to erupt on the other side. I pushed it wider and wider, inch by frightful inch, until I could see the staircase in front of me. The air was clear, and the stairs were empty. There was no sound from above or below, so I stepped in, and it felt calm in comparison with what I was leaving. Until a smell hit me, vitriol in vapor form. It filled my throat, and I choked. *There must be a fire*, I thought, even though the stench was the only sign of it.

Growing up in Bellevue in the Pines Apartments, I saw many fires. I remember one night when my brother Paul had a friend sleeping over, the fire alarm went off, shocking us all out of sleep. Everyone got up, and Paul made each of us carry out a piece of his brand-new Apple computer, his technological pride and joy. I walked out wearing my pajamas and clutching a disk drive for dear life, the smell of charred wood and melted plastic inescapable. My friend Cherry's apartment was the one that was burning. They lost everything that day.

The smoke in this stairway smelled different. It was corrosive, eating at my lungs with every breath, invisible and insidious. It singed my throat. It was strong enough that whatever was burning, fire would soon follow. I had too much to live for. I could not lose everything that day. *Run*, said a small voice. And then louder: *RUN!*

I gripped the railing, focusing on coordinating my feet with the steps, my hands with the slope of the stairs. From the landing, I jumped down the steps, landing on my left foot in the middle of the flight. Grabbing the railing tightly but briefly, I sprang off, landing with my right foot on the landing this time. I took a second step, then again— *step, step, jump.* One more flight, one more landing, one more floor. *Step, step, jump.*

I had never sprinted so fast, the air clearer and my hope stronger with each leap. I was flying, and I felt powerful like each step was a statement—*I will make it out. I will get out of this alive.*

As each floor passed—45, 41, 36 —I began to see people entering the stairwell from the floors I was sprinting past. I heard a man yell out behind me.

"Slow down, sweetheart! Don't hurt yourself!" He had fear in his voice, but all I could think was: *why isn't he running?*

I reached the 33rd floor and stopped short, my momentum halted by a sudden mass. People filed along the right side of the stairwell in a perfect, straight line, unmoving and seemingly unaware of what was waiting above us. I was petrified, impatient with their deference to order and their insistence on politeness.

"Why aren't you moving??" I cried out.

"Everything's going to be fine," said a man next to me as though I were complaining about a long line at the cafeteria. "Everyone's going as fast as possible."

I was dumbfounded—these same people would sprint like mad to squeeze themselves into subway cars every morning and afternoon, but they fell into rank when they should have been running for their lives.

"What about the left side of the stairs?" I yelled. "How can you just stand there?"

"The firemen," he said solemnly. "They need room to come up."

Why would the firemen be heading up, I thought *when everyone is trying to get out of the building?*

It was a pedestrian gridlock. No one spoke. We all stood, breathing in the astringent air. I took the sweater I had plucked off the back of my chair just minutes ago and pressed it against my nose. I tried to stay calm on the outside to counter the creeping frenzy inside of me—patience felt like a critical mistake, but we were packed.

A few steps ahead of me was a young Puerto Rican guy with baggy jeans that hung off his birdlike build. His two-way pager chirped.

A woman asked him, "Have you heard anything?"

He nodded. "A plane hit the tower."

"A plane?" I yelled.

He nodded again. "A passenger plane. A big one."

I looked up at the ceiling of the floor above me and started to pray. *Dear God, please keep this building upright. Please keep the plane from falling down on us.*

I peered over the railing, panic rising. "Why aren't we moving?"

"Firemen are on their way up!" came a voice from below.

For a brief moment, I was comforted—help was coming. But what could even the bravest of men do to battle a burning jet?

I tried to calm myself anyway, but the stench was overwhelming. I looked around and saw someone I knew, a security guard who would always look my way and say hello when I'd happen to pass him in the hallways. He was always predictably flirtatious, looking at me with a faint twinkle as we passed.

He looked at me now, but if he found any solace in seeing a familiar face, it didn't show.

"Is there any other way out?" I asked him. "What are they saying on the walkie-talkie?" I motioned to the device on his hip.

Everyone around us turned to look. His eyes found mine, but the spark of recognition I thought I would find there seemed to have been snuffed out and replaced instead with shock. He looked beyond me, through me, as he reached down and turned the knob on his walkie, slowly distinguishing the soft murmur of sound. It clicked off, silenced, and I turned away.

We were stopped, and it seemed like forever. I started to hear murmurs from the people around me, pulling out small snippets— *Tower 2, impact, an airplane.*

"What's happening?" I asked.

"Tower 2 was hit," said the Puerto Rican man.

"With what?" I asked.

"Another plane," said a stranger. "This wasn't an accident."

They say you can smell fear, an odorless chemical that rises off people under stress and duress, a signal that your brain can instantly recognize. At that moment, and forever after that day, the smell of fear is and will forever be instantly recognizable to me: sharp, like red-hot metal, twisted and strained; musty, like a basement after a deep rain; toxic, choking ash; the potpourri of the lives people brought in with them on that day—their perfume, their last meal, their habits, their family, their hope, their mistakes. We all realized the same truth together: *we were being attacked.*

"Move to the side! Injured coming down!" someone yelled.

I saw her arms first, waving and whipping, fingers clutching at anything she could find—metal rails, a stranger's tensed shoulder, the air itself. She was trembling, gasping for air, her green silk blouse swaying with every short breath. Whatever she had seen, it haunted her.

Behind her walked a zombie, someone who that morning had been a healthy girl in her mid-twenties but who was now scorched and stained. Her clothes were gone, but knitted sweaters were knotted around her bare waist and another around her back, her bra intact. A gray-green foam covered her head and shoulders. Blisters had erupted on her chest and back. Her blonde hair was black with flame, and her skin hung in charred sheets off her limbs.

They passed us, seemingly in slow motion, and I could suddenly picture how it all unfolded—the young woman sitting at her desk; the plane crashing through the walls; her coworker in the green silk blouse watching her burn. And it hit me all at once, the magnitude of what was happening, the gravity of the situation we were in.

I looked up, and an older man with bright blue eyes looked at me kindly. "Everything is going to be alright," he said, perhaps as much for himself as for me. I took comfort in it. I so desperately wanted to believe him.

There came more calls of "move to the right!" and a fireman came running up dressed in the full black gear striped with yellow and carrying a hatchet in his hand. He was flanked by dozens of his fellow rescue workers, who flooded up the staircase as fast as they could with picks, axes, and hoses. I had known they were on their way, but the timing seemed wrong.

"Why are they coming here now?" I asked, panicked, to no one in particular. "They should let all the people out before they head up! How will they ever get out?"

I was the only voice in the stairs. No one, civilian or rescue crew, could answer me.

Their red hats had a #9 emblazoned on them, and they all looked strong, tall, and stoic. One of them even looked beautiful. He had light skin and dark hair, with eyes the color of a clear sky. The line he was walking in stopped inches from me, and we regarded each other. When I looked at him, I found the answer to my question—I expected to see fear in his eyes, or bravery, or even anger. But what I saw instead was acceptance.

He knew that each step was a countdown to the inevitable, that it was his job to climb directly into fear without faltering. A sob caught in my throat, tripped up by the unfairness of it all. He knew the terror that would meet him at the top of the tower, and he somehow still found the power to put one boot in front of the next. He stared back at me, reluctant tears threatening to spill out onto his dust-stained cheek. We had never met and would never meet again, but in that moment, we ceased to be strangers, bonded together by the sharp cut of common consciousness.

And then he was gone, the line had moved, our connection severed. And instead of feeling afraid, which seemed like a rational reaction, I was overwhelmed with despair. We were on the 27th floor, and in all my months in that building, the ground had never felt so very far away.

I peered down the stairs—no firemen, just an empty lane—and within seconds, I was running again. *Step, step, jump.* One floor, then two, then two more. When a fireman came up, I would tuck myself back into line to let them pass, but otherwise, I flew as fast as I possibly could.

"Stay on the right side!" yelled a woman.

As a girl, I had always followed the rules, always done the right thing, a habit that had followed me into adulthood. But even I had my limits. I was struck with the same spirit that grabbed me when my hand punched through the windshield years before. *I-don't-care-what-people-think.*

"You do not get to tell me what to do," I snapped at her. "I will go wherever the fuck I want to go! I am *not* dying here!"

Everyone turned, shocked at the language or the honesty, but I was just as shocked that they were all just standing there complacent, not fighting to get out, not able to help themselves.

I looked up to a sign that read *17th Floor*, and I could finally hear fire alarms sounding as we passed by closed doors. When they opened, people joining our escapist ranks, smoke poured in. It was heavy and cloying, and it threatened to overtake us.

A man in a blue suit came into view, heavyset with dark brown hair, sweat dripping down from his head to his face, which was red as a ripe strawberry. He could barely breathe.

"There is an area … on the 10th floor … where you can get some fresh air," he said. "If you need to, take a break and continue walking down… whenever you feel better."

He seemed delusional—who in their right mind would choose to spend more time in this building than absolutely necessary? But the woman next to me, dressed in a black blazer and black jeans with a laptop hanging from her shoulder, all but raised her hand.

"I definitely need to get some air," she said. She was the only one. I desperately hoped she'd reconsider.

Floor 14. A bunch of firemen were gathered. They'd propped the door of the stairwell open, and I heard the smash of glass breaking— they'd taken the butt of an axe to break a vending machine and were handing out bottles of water.

Looking past the open doorway into the hallway, two firemen remained there, drinking water and talking—a quiet one, young and boyish-looking but serious, and the other, tall and lanky and blond.

The tall one, the towhead, was laughing. "Man, this mother is going *down*!" he shrieked, seemingly gleeful at the prospect of all that chaos. His partner saw me watching and looked away, embarrassed, perhaps, or frightened because he thought the same.

The lady in black with the laptop pushed past me.

"I need some air *now*," she said. She looked at me. "Anybody want to come?"

I shook my head no but couldn't speak. She walked past the doorway and onto that floor, a march toward what seemed to be an inescapable fate. I wanted to tell her to turn around, to come down with the rest of us, but she was already gone. I never saw her again.

It was time to move again. Using the left-hand passing lane, I sprinted down a whole flight before I spotted a man in blue with a rag over his mouth, a walkie-talkie hovering just in front of his face.

"Do you work here?" I asked. He nodded. "Is there another way to get out?" I asked.

"No, but you'll get out the way you're going," he said, his voice confident. "And when you do, go wherever they tell you to go. Look straight ahead. There is a lot of... debris. There are things you don't want to see. When you get out of the building, get as far away from this place as possible."

Along with the crowd, I siphoned down the stairwell as far and as fast as we could. We hit the 10th floor. There was water everywhere, the sprinklers still flowing at full speed. Water was rolling down the steps, little waterfalls cascading underfoot. I weaved in and out of the crowd—step, step, jump; step, step, jump.

The stairway ended in a nondescript doorway that opened to a long corridor. But instead of relief to be out of that enclosed space, I felt an immense pressure weighing on me from above and spurring me from behind. I was drenched, shifting my cardigan from a makeshift mask to an insufficient blanket over my shoulders. I was freezing, even though the building was warm, but forward movement was the only feeling I cared enough to think about.

We made our way to the lobby in darkness. The fixtures had fallen from the ceilings and walls, and the lightbulbs had burst. The lobby was half a foot underwater, the bustling hub I had seen that morning had been abandoned and destroyed. I kept my head down, my eyes straight, and even though every part of me was saying I should leave through the front entrance—the closest to air, the most direct route—I followed the man with the blue rag's instructions. Out of the corner of my eyes, I could see signs of what he had warned me to avoid—chunks of our building, still smoking; a splash of crimson splattered against the front windows; the chaos of people lost, found, and fighting.

We were ushered through a revolving door and out into the adjacent mall, past The Coffee Station, which always had lines out the door each morning. It was empty now, dark and eerie and aching. I walked as fast as I could, thankful for the Easy Spirit ankle boots I'd put on in a hurry that morning. I walked by a woman struggling through puddles in slip-on heels, and I wondered which floor I'd still be on if I had worn those instead.

Go, go, go, past Menchanko-Tei, where I'd get Japanese food when I had the taste for it and the time. Past Ecce Panis, the bakery where I'd buy rich pastries to reward myself and take long sips of perfect cappuccinos. And then, finally and mercifully, up the escalators and into Borders Books.

Rushing past the aisles of self-help and stacks of bestsellers, I pushed through the doors to the outside world and gulped in the fresh air. It caught in my lungs, so desperate I was for oxygen. A woman in uniform was directing us, repeating in a clear, loud voice: "Please walk across the street and clear the area!"

I did as she asked, crossing Greenwich Street and onto Cortland along with the streaming crowd. Once I was safely on the other side, I turned around and looked up. Tower 2 was engulfed in flames, and fire was bursting out of both sides of Tower 1. I had seen enough, been through enough, to know the devastation had only just begun.

I stood, visually tracing the steps I had taken to make my way out, my eyes sketching the path on the outside of the building where inside I had skipped and scraped my way to the bottom. Where I hustled through the corridor, into the lobby, across the mall, and finally onto the sweetest surface: solid ground.

The blaze seemed to brush the clouds, streaming all the way up to the sky, reducing these dual pillars into fragile things, kindling for hell and hatred.

"Dear God," I whimpered, my hand over my mouth. It was as much an exclamation as it was a prayer.

The smoke screamed toward the Brooklyn Bridge, and I fought the urge to put one foot in front of the other, *step, step, jump, step, step, jump*, for miles until I reached my refuge in the Bronx.

I wondered for a moment if the crows were still cawing outside my window or if they were silent now, their prophecy fulfilled.

And then I did the only thing I could think of—I put my back to the towers and ran.

4

Church Street Smoke

I ran, the crackle and sizzle of the escaping flames quieter with every step. The sound of the sirens whirred around me, a deafening clamor. But the towers were like a beacon, and my quaking legs begged to stop. I slowed, paused, and turned around to look back at the building.

I reached into my purse and grabbed a disposable camera, a piece of promotional gear I had picked up in the past few weeks. I looked up and snapped a picture, a slice of living history, as though the memory wouldn't be forever etched into my mind, as though my nightmares weren't all but guaranteed to play the scene on repeat.

All around me, people were flowing in the wrong direction, pulled to the burning buildings like mindless moths propelled by awe and disbelief. I wanted to shout at them to run, that nothing good would be found there, but I found I barely had the energy to stay standing, let alone scream out, let alone send out a warning.

I turned to put more distance between me and the tower. I pulled out my cellphone—was my family safe? My brother Paul worked across the connecting bridge from the Trade Center to the World Financial

Center. He could have easily crossed over. What about my dad in Seattle or my mom in New York? Had they heard the news? Were they worrying? I was desperate to speak to someone I loved, to get word to them that I was okay and to reassure myself of the same.

The line was busy, a constant beep beep beep in my ear as I walked. My feet moved faster with each failed call. I was heading north as fast as I could on Broadway, in the general direction of the Bronx, so strong was the pull to get back to my home, my sanctuary. I wanted out of the city. I needed as much distance between myself and this moment as possible.

With each step, tears came rushing down. Slowly, I began to realize the state I was in. My clothes were drenched from the sprinkler system. My pants were soaking wet. My boots were drenched, a slurry of water and chemicals. I shuddered, thinking about what I had to step through.

The tears would not stop. Every call that wouldn't go through, every step I took, every breath that rattled through my lungs and acrid stench that swept through my nose were reminders of how close I had come to death. Then, out of nowhere:

"Are you okay, miss?" A light-skinned woman with bright red hair and Coke bottle glasses approached me. She knew I wasn't all right. "Can I walk with you?"

She held my arm tightly, gently but firmly. She offered me a tissue. I looked down to see she had a plastic Duane Reade bag full of them.

"Have you been able to contact your mother?"

"My phone isn't working!" I cried.

"I'm Patty," she offered as a response. "I'm going to help you however I can."

Walking together, we passed a line of dozens queued up. A few steps later, we realized they were all waiting in line to use a payphone. The sun beat down on us all. At the front of the line, the woman on the payphone mashed on the keys.

"Do you want to call your mother?" asked Patty.

I shook my head *no*.

"I can't wait that long," I replied. "I have to get out of here."

But there everyone else stood, crowds of people with their eyes on the towers, dazed and delirious from the heat and hellish scene in front of them. Around us, people shambled around slowly like zombies free of purpose, unclear of destination.

We finally reached Broadway and Canal.

"N or R train, hon?" Patty asked me kindly.

I panicked. "No way, I cannot be underground," I told her in fright.

Mercifully, we spotted a cab across the street and hurried across Canal together just as an Asian family of four poured out. *Yes,* I thought, but as I reached for the door, a man in a dark gray suit flung it open and stepped inside. He had solid blue eyes, like circles of ice, and perfectly combed brown hair. Tears streaming down my face, I looked at him sitting right in front of the window, and he looked up at me, emotionless.

He shook his head slowly no. I shivered. This man felt empty, soulless, sinister, so I stepped back and let him roll away.

A minute later, another cab crept up to where we were standing, and Patty stepped up to the doorway. I was too rattled.

"Would you mind sharing this cab with her?" she asked.

The guy inside immediately scooted over and said, "Sure." I stepped up, asked him where he was going, and he said he was heading up to 86th Street on the eastside. Close enough. I climbed in and scooted over so Patty could join us. She just stood there.

"Aren't you coming with us?"

"No, hon, I'm going to take a bus. I'm headed to the other side of town anyway," she said with a sweet smile. As desperate as I was to leave, I hopped out and gave her a huge hug. She handed me her card, which I tucked into my soggy purse, and we pulled away.

I looked up to the cabbie, a dark-skinned man with a serious look.

"Thank you for stopping for me," I said.

He nodded in return. I turned to the man sitting beside me and extended my arm in greeting.

"I'm Annabel."

"I'm Anthony," he replied. His hand felt warm in mine.

The cab was a refuge, an escape hatch on wheels. But it couldn't move fast enough. My urge to get home was so strong yet was met by immovable traffic going west on Canal Street. We inched closer to the intersection of Canal and Church, waiting as the light refused to turn green and let us pass.

The people outside seemed unaware of what was happening just blocks away from them. Everyone was milling around, going about their days, doing business as usual.

"Why aren't they moving?" I asked Anthony.

"Why aren't *we* moving?" he asked back, sharing my anxiety to get as far from the towers as possible.

"It's mesmerizing, I guess," I said quietly. "As long as you didn't just have to sprint down 46 floors to get out of there."

I looked up at him, his face itself a kindness, warm and open and strong.

Out of the corner of my eye, I saw the light finally turned green. We approached the intersection of Church and Canal, but our progress stalled.

"Let's go!" I yelled at the cab driver, my fear taking over. "Can we please hurry up?"

"I can't," he said, the strong African voice barely a whisper. "Look at the people."

I heard them first, a billow of screams. Then I saw them, a veritable stampede, hundreds of people running on each other's heels and tumbling toward us. People dashed directly into the intersection, in front of cars, over one another, just looking for a refuge from the ashen assailant behind them. From inside the cab, we could only watch, horrified, as people weaved in and out of traffic, some directly into the paths of oncoming cars.

Anthony and I were desperate to see what was happening—what was coming, what we might need to do in response. What were they running from? Did we have to jump out to join with them? What did we need to do to survive?

I opened the car door slightly, peeking through the crack. What was my move?

"Don't get out!" he yelled, grabbing my hand.

"Young lady, close the door *now*!" yelled the cab driver.

I shut it, my mind having been made up for me. The cab driver locked the door.

"Look," he said, pointing from the front seat through the windshield.

And then we saw it, a white cloud several stories high, tall enough that it seemed to engulf the sky itself. It barreled toward us, threatening to swallow us whole.

"What is it?" I asked, the panic rising in my throat. It was white like smoke, but I had never seen anyone run that fast from fumes.

As the cloud hit each building in its path, it grew even taller. It sounded like it was growling, rushing toward us at a furious pace. The crowd was overrun in seconds, the smoke devouring them whole. They couldn't be seen, but we could still hear their screams, even as the cloud swallowed us, too.

Fleeing men and women darted all around us. We saw some desperately running up stoops to try to break into doorways. A man passed by us and wrenched on my door handle, his fist pounding against the window when it wouldn't budge.

The cab driver locked the doors again. "I am not picking up any more people!"

I looked at Anthony, the horror playing on both of our faces.

"Do you think it's another attack?" I asked.

"A bomb?" he questioned.

But all I could think of was something else, something I had grown up believing in, preparing for, and knowing was an eventual inevitability.

"I used to dream of this as a little girl," I said to Anthony.

"Of an attack?"

I shook my head *no*. "Of the end times," I said. "This is exactly what I always thought it would look like—chaos, an inferno, people running everywhere, smoke in our lungs."

"What does that mean, Annabel?" he asked, and I noticed his knuckles were white from grabbing the door handle so tightly.

What does it mean? I asked myself. Memories poured over me. Even though I was in the cab, my mind was elsewhere.

My childhood had prepared me for this. Raised as a Seventh-Day Adventist, I grew up with those words in my ears, spoken by the brothers and sisters of the church. Growing up with that faith shaped a large part of who I am. Seventh-Day Adventists, a type of Protestant-Judaic Christianity, keep the 10 commandments by observing Sabbath Friday sundown to Saturday sundown. We go to church on Saturdays.

We usually do not eat meat, drink, or smoke, we do not wear jewelry, we believe in the second coming of Jesus Christ.

"*Estamos en los ultimos tiempos,*" I remembered hearing in church as a young girl. *We are in the end of days.*

I remember one day being in the foyer, playing outside of the church sanctuary. Sister Betanzos, a slender and strong Michoacan woman, would always tell us, "The church is not for playing, children. We are here to glorify God. Get back inside."

I did as she asked that day, sneaking back into the sermon to listen to the pastor, a tall elderly man who was strong and patient.

He began with, "*Nuestro Dios, que estas en los cielos,*" the familiar words, *Our God, who art in heaven.* He asked us to pray, not for salvation, nor for peace, but to prepare for the second coming of Jesus Christ. Adventists believe in a literal second coming of Jesus that he will return to the Earth and the faithful will meet him in the sky on their way to heaven.

Some of the biggest lessons the pastor taught us were practical: where we should go, what we should bring, what places would be safe after Jesus returned, and which would fall to sin. Cities were foretold to be one of the most dangerous places of all.

Fire was a key tenet of the prophecy. In scripture, Paul tells us "the Lord Jesus [will be] revealed from heaven in blazing fire with his powerful angels" (2 Thessalonians 1:7). And Peter joins him in saying, "The heavens will disappear with a roar," and the Earth will be burned up (2 Peter 3:10).

When this happens, the faithful must be prepared to leave the cities as they would become hotbeds of sin and fire, with food unfit to eat and air unfit to breathe.

Looking out from the cab at the smoke that surrounded us, the lessons of my childhood came roaring back to me. The end of times was

a topic of constant speculation, the leaders and congregants
hypothesizing at how bad things were in the world, how lost people
were, how Jesus must be coming soon to reward the righteous. I learned
about Daniel reading dreams, about how the formation of empires and
the clay and steel crumbling, about the seven plagues, about the origins
of the Sabbath in Dominican law.

I am grateful for my Adventist faith, for the benefits of observing the
Sabbath every week. I was taught to be "in the world and not of the
world." I learned how to be comfortable with time alone and to use that
time to connect directly with God. It was very difficult—it took a lot of
discipline at a young age, and my parents were very strict. On the
Sabbath, we weren't allowed to play with friends or partake in
extracurricular activities. Even Saturday morning cartoons weren't
allowed. They taught us that God was always watching, and every time I
tried to sneak into the living room to watch cartoons, I learned my
parents were always watching, too.

To prepare for the Sabbath, we cleaned the house, my mom cooked
extra food, and my brother Paul would make his awesome whole wheat
bread. Cooking wasn't allowed on Sabbath, so we would snack all day or
warm up the food we had cooked the night before. Altogether, we'd
have a "culto," a short time for worship to honor the beginning of the
Sabbath. We'd sing hymns, Paul would read from the Bible and lead us
in prayer, and if we were lucky, he would practice his parable in front of
us before he'd perform it in front of the church.

He was truly gifted. He and our cousin Dennis would recite
parables, but it wasn't a simple reading—it was a spoken word
interpretation of a lesson from the Bible that they would memorize and
bring to life through their performance. My favorite was when Paul was
the narrator, Dennis was Joseph, and Cecilia, the most beautiful girl at
church, with cinnamon skin, silky long black hair, and the biggest,

brightest smile, played Mary. That story had never sounded so good! Those three were the youth leaders of our church and spent time at both the American and Latino churches since we all shared the same building.

Church leaders spent a lot of time on youth education, the parables they performed reinforcing the lessons we all learned during the pastor's sermons. We were taught a great deal about the superiority and rightness of the Seventh-Day Adventist church, especially when it came to man's laws vs. God's laws. Adventists obeyed all of God's 10 commandments, while other faiths, we were told, picked and chose different ideas and laws with the purpose of serving men's needs.

It seemed critical that the younger generation understand this difference. As Adventists, we did the best job of observing all of God's commandments, not just the ones that were convenient or cultivated favor and power. We were taught that God does not change, and because of that, we cannot change his laws.

But there was one part of the church's teachings that had never made sense to me, that never seemed to be of divine origin. Adventists believed that dancing was a sin. Dancing, the thing I loved so much, the center of so much of my life to date.

Back in the cab, I said to Anthony: "Dancing."

"What does dancing have to do with the end times?" he asked.

"Seventh-Day Adventists forbid dancing."

"How does that work, exactly?"

"Not particularly well for me," I joked, my mind steeling itself against the chaos outside by focusing on the memories within.

I was 15 when I realized that church-taught approaches to challenges could be wrong. In Ecuadorian and Latino culture, a young woman's 15th birthday is a big rite of passage. She has Quinceañera, a big party to celebrate her transition to womanhood. This day usually involves going to church, speaking publicly as a way to introduce yourself officially, and paradoxically for me, learning and dancing the waltz.

As Adventists, that wasn't allowed, but dancing was a core part of Latino culture. Latino dancing is a mélange of African music and dance (Yuka) meets Spanish colonial clave into the forever changing rumba, which now resembles a polite and respectful salsa dance that we all do.

Just like our dancing had historical roots, the Adventist prohibition of dancing stemmed from the colonial cultural dominance of the Western church leaders over the indigenous and African people in the 1800s. It was seen as primitive, sexual, a way for them to rise up against their captors. Outlawing dancing was a way to oppress people even further, to strip them of their culture in order to fully control them. It was, quite simply, a law of men.

That knowledge, the comfort we had in knowing that God wasn't actually against physical expression set to music, made it easy to think we could have both: our church and our culture. But that wasn't to be.

We planned for the Quinceañera for months—I remember my dress, mi padrinos, the food, the decorations, the invitations, my mom cooking all night, her asking a friend to host it at her beautiful home in Newport Bellevue. I remember inviting my principal and his wife. My friends from school and my cousins were the caballeros and damas of the party, my Quinceañera court.

On the day of, I remember all my uncles dressed in tuxedos. Tio Joaquin had given me the dress. Tio Cesar had provided the deejay. Tio David paid for the cake. My dad and my mom handled everything else, all the plans and all the details. It was a true group effort, a real family affair. Even my sister Carol and her baby, my cute *sobrino* Bryan came. We hadn't seen each other for a year and a half, so being able to see her face after so long was a balm on a wound that hadn't healed.

In fact, seeing her at my Quinceañera was the greatest gift I received that day. We never addressed the reason behind not speaking for so long, but she came to show her love, and I got to see my nephew again. Sometimes someone's presence is all the apology you need. I couldn't believe the feeling of euphoria, the relief in being reunited, and how, for the first time in such a long time, it felt like we had a chance to have a future together as a family.

When it was time to begin, my brother Paul, dressed to the nines in his tuxedo, took my arm. Together, we walked down the huge staircase, he gave me to our father, and he officially started the festivities with a heartfelt and amazing speech. I said a few words, thanked everyone for coming, and then he whisked me onto the dance floor, where everyone danced the waltz together. I was so happy. The dancing, the tradition, all the ways we were able to bring the Latino culture to my small Seventh-Day Adventist Pacific Northwestern world. It was a truly diverse room, with people from all around the world coming together to celebrate and share in the joy of becoming a young woman.

But that feeling didn't last.

"Can you believe that our church was so upset with my mom and our whole family for just dancing? And for having a little alcohol at the party?" I said to Anthony.

"I can't believe it," he replied softly, looking out the window. It was hard to tell whether he was talking about my memory or about the world just outside the cab.

After the party, my mother was called to sit in front of the committee of discipline, *la junta*, the jury. She was all alone, taking all the blame, made to sit in front of an assembly of congregants and church leaders, scolded for not following the rules even though she wasn't the one who was breaking them. They chastised her, calling her out for having a party, for the alcohol that was at the party, dancing, and celebrating. They didn't understand that my parents were divorced and my dad planned the party not in the "Adventist" way. It was so hard to go from the highs of that moment, the healing that occurred in our family, just to see the church come down and truly destroy what was so good for bringing all of us together.

They listed her sins one by one, a rap sheet of what we had gone wrong. But all I could think of were their wrongdoings: their hypocrisy, their internal racism, the cultural bias, and their unkind and uncompassionate hearts.

It was the first fissure in my faith with the church, in the institution itself, in the men who ran it and used it to further their own purposes. Thankfully, it did nothing to rupture my belief in God. It deepened it. I saw the juxtaposition of man's laws with God's grace. The latter is eternal, a bigger and bolder force than man's edicts.

"If this were the second coming," I said in the cab, "there would only be one thing to do."

"We've got to get out of here," said the driver, answering my prompt. He swerved just enough to find a pathway around the car that stopped ahead of us. We were able to make slow, steady progress west on Canal until we finally got to 6th Avenue, The Avenue of the Americas, to make a right going north.

That meant two things: one, we were finally making progress north, toward home, and two, we finally had an unobstructed view of the towers I had so recently escaped from. We turned around in our seats to look back at them. My tower, the North Tower, was still burning, flames & smoke shooting out from all sides. But, unbelievably, the South Tower was completely gone.

"My God," said Anthony, his hand to his mouth.

A sob escaped me, the only reply I was capable of. Tears slipped down my cheeks of their own accord.

The cab driver crossed himself but did not take his eyes off the open wound in the sky.

"The people!" I yelled. "There were so many people inside of there still."

"The smoke," said Anthony somberly. "The tower falling must have caused all the white smoke."

I choked on the air, the pulverized concrete and the remains of those lost all mixed together. We fell apart together, we wept for them, for their lives, for their families, for their souls, and for the futures they woke up with that morning.

How could this be? How could the tower have fallen? What if I had stayed under my desk like I had wanted to? What if I had followed that woman in the stairwell who was clutching her laptop to the deck for some fresh air? And did that man in the office next to me, the one who stood in the doorway, ever get out? It could have easily been me.

I had made it out of the building but knowing the tower had fallen and looking out the window to the clouded air that hung over the city, I couldn't help but feel like a catastrophe was still near. It felt like my spirit was still aflame.

"Go!" I yelled, my whole body clenched and filled with the need to get out of the city, to make my way home. Our wheels inched forward. Inside the cab, we were silent. But outside, the silence was broken by the sounds of screams and sirens.

"Go," I whimpered, remembering a verse from the Book of Revelations: *They threw dust on their heads and kept crying out, weeping, and mourning, Woe, woe, the great city... for in a single hour she was destroyed.*

5

Saint Anthony

My breath forced its way through my lungs in sharp gasps, small little sips of air that provided shallow comfort. They came quickly, *inout, inout, inout.* I folded over at the waist to cradle my heavy head in my hands as though the support might redirect the necessary energy to my lungs.

Inout, inout, inout.

Questions ricocheted through my head, rattling around in every corner of my aching muscles and shaking bones. *Who could do such a thing? Why me? Why now? What was going to happen to us? Where would they attack next? What had I done to deserve this?*

The air passed in and out faster, and my vision started to darken at the edges. One question remained: *Why did they want to kill me?*

Just as the remaining light before me started to fade, squeezed out by panic, I felt a hand on my shoulder.

"Breathe," said Anthony softly beside me. "Slow it down. Just breathe." Slowly, my lungs opened up, and my mind settled enough that the thoughts came a bit quieter, a bit less quickly. I found an equilibrium, a place of stillness as I drew on what felt like my last reservoirs of strength.

"Thank you," I said to him, my heart no longer racing.

He nodded and smiled kindly.

"We have to take care of each other," he said softly.

It shouldn't have been a radical concept, the basic care for others. Anthony and I were strangers, and yet he had found the humanity in his heart to both comfort and connect with me. What made the opposite also true? What made people turn their backs on each other, lash out at a stranger, destroy buildings, take lives, punish the world? When we could so easily be an "us," what turned people into a "them?"

"What is happening out there?" asked Anthony, his face pressed to the window, watching the chaos unfold on the streets, the people walking around in a daze.

"It's wild," I replied because that's what it looked like, all the trappings of civility stripped away.

I felt palpably vulnerable, my whole body a soft spot.

"I can't stop thinking about the people who are still up there," I said.

"Me, too," Anthony replied.

"If I hadn't listened to my intuition, to God, if I hadn't sprinted down those stairs, who knows where I would be right now."

"I know," he said, taking a deep breath of his own. "I was working on the top of the Federal Reserve Building."

"What do you do?" I asked.

"I work construction. Or I guess I used to … I might be fired."

"What happened?"

"It was a pretty routine job, actually, until the tower got hit. But even though we could see it was bad news, my supervisor wouldn't let us leave. I walked out on my own. Judging by what he yelled at me as I left, he didn't exactly appreciate that."

"I am sure they'll understand," I assured him.

He shrugged. "And to think, that's not even close to the worst thing that's happened today."

As I looked out the window, I struggled to process it all. My clothes were soaked and soot-stained. The smell of the burning buildings, two bonfires blazing in the sky, was inescapable. There was so much I couldn't wrap my head around—who was still trapped in the building, how they were going to get out, what was going to happen to my job, whether or not Mr. Lin got out okay, what my family must be thinking, and so much more. But there was one question that rang through my mind louder than the others.

"Why do you think they wanted to kill us?" I asked Anthony.

He was silent for a long stretch of time.

Then he whispered, "I don't know. I can't imagine what kind of life would lead to thinking this was your only option."

He couldn't imagine, but I desperately wanted to. I searched for answers, aching for reasons to answer that question. I struggled to reason with the assumption that our lives simply didn't matter to them.

There in that cab, inching our way uptown, I thought through everything I had ever learned about the way the world worked. I sifted through memory, through lessons, through reading and experiences as one would pan for gold: desperately searching for a nugget of comprehension. If I could understand them, I could make sense of the attack. If I could empathize with them, see beyond their sin and into their souls, I could move past the panic. Without understanding, it would be a senseless act, and that scared me more than anything.

Years earlier, men had tried to bomb that iconic building to bring down this shining emblem of the Western world. They had failed, though not without consequence. Lives were lost, our national sense of security faltered, business suffered—and yet, we rebuilt.

If the people flying those planes were in a similar mindset or had similar reasoning, then at least in their own fractured minds, the destruction made sense.

"They weren't after us," I said softly, almost to myself.

"Then what were they after?"

"I would bet they were after what those buildings stand for."

Whoever was in those planes, whoever took their own lives to make some sort of statement, must have felt that whatever casualties ensued were collateral damage. They didn't see me, or any of the living, breathing people in the World Trade Center—they saw the United States government. They saw a mechanism of oppression. They saw a force in need of reckoning.

I loved my country, but I often felt ashamed of our collective history. In a way, I sympathized, not with what the men flying the planes had done, but with the broken hearts they must have been carrying inside of them their whole lives. To have lived a life of marginalization, oppression, and compromised futures is to have lived a half-life.

Yet, just like with all questions, as I stirred and tried to find meaning, I found mostly half-truths. My life, my memories, and everything I had ever read or learned about history, politics, and culture just poured out of me, gushing like a waterfall.

I grappled with why some societies were pitted against each other, the atrocities of the acts of governments, and the hatred that can bloom within a soul and transform planes into bombs. There is no separating the acts of our government from the acts of our own. I realized that I almost died and that other people in the towers had actually lost their lives, all because of those in power and how they chose to use it.

But that does not abdicate us of our own responsibility. We can't say we didn't know what was happening around the world because even if that's true, the fact is that our ignorance is a choice. We choose not to know. We choose not to care. We choose to focus on what we want, to support our lifestyle, and we don't do anything to rectify historical wrongs, which allows us to just continue compounding the harm.

What future had those people been robbed of? In what ways had they been denied their human rights? How have the decisions of our leaders had a negative impact on their lives? How was the current system of the world stacked against them?

"You know what I was thinking about just before the plane hit?"

Anthony shook his head.

"A global minimum wage. What do you think that would do to the world?"

"It's a little out of my lane," he said sheepishly. "You work in finance. Do you think it's a good idea?"

"For multinational companies, absolutely," I said, thinking of the 50% of the world's people who subsist on less than $10 a day. "In many ways, it seems like the least we could do."

I thought about the sins of our country, of capitalism, of Western civilization as a whole that I am a part of. I thought about the economic and environmental injustice.

"We make up 10% of the global population, but we use 45% of the world's resources. Did you know that? So just by living this way, we are making 90% of the world's population fight for the remaining 55% of resources. It doesn't take a mathematician to see that if you X out that 10% of the population, 90% of the people could live and divide all the world's resources," thinking, maybe this is why I almost got X out. "And I love this country—don't get me wrong—but Western society is a selfish society. So many are suffering, and yet we take and take and take. This is why we need multinational corporations to stop acting like a bunch of lawless conquistadors and pay a global minimum wage. How much longer will we as people, not just of America but of the world, continue to look the other way?"

"Maybe this will be a wake-up call," Anthony suggested.

And for me, in many ways, it already was. As I thought of the fallen towers, the white plume, the shaking walls, and shattered windows, I was struck by this truth: every material that goes into a building is only good when it's upright. The moment a building falls, there is no use for all the wood, all that metal, glass, rugs, lights, desks, and doors. Then, it's simply turns into garbage and returns to Mother Earth.

"I can't believe it's gone," I said.

"Me either," replied Anthony.

"This structure that I felt was so powerful was just pulverized into smithereens. Humans really don't make a damn thing."

"What do you mean?" he asked.

"We take everything from Mother Earth, and we change it, shift it, transform it, but it's still not made by us. We can't make wood, we can't make rock, steel, glass, none of it. We only make humans and ideas. That's it.

"Everything else, we just take from her, and she gets nothing back, not even a thank you. Not care, not respect, nothing except extraction for our perceived notions of value, for the human construct we call 'money.' But money doesn't mean much when you're burning, when your life is in the balance, or when you're at war. You can't buy time. You can't buy life. You can't buy peace."

"No, we can't, can we?" Anthony said, his face stoic. He let out a huge sigh.

We held the silence together. My mind, still a whirl of ideas and justifications, of rage and disbelief, was grappling with the way we treat the Earth. If the root of this attack was resources, if it was the fight over capitalism and its root, money, then are we letting paradigms elude the reality of this life?

When the Europeans traversed the Western hemisphere, they took with them three tons of gold and over 16,000 tons of silver. Before that, trade and barter were the currency. Money is a concept, a creation, not an absolute. And value is a shifting proposition. The plain truth is that if Mother Earth didn't give us natural silver or gold to us, we would not be able to physically have tangible money for everyone. We wouldn't be able to sell it or buy it or use it.

We lie to ourselves and believe those lies because there is a theory, a whole system that supports it, and we think we will never have to reckon with that truth.

"Maybe we could create a fund for Mother Earth," I mused out loud.

"What do you mean?" Anthony asked.

"Maybe we could create a small transactional percentage fee for each trade on all global commodity platforms to benefit the planet? So that the money would sustain communities, benefit the land, and help indigenous people around the world? We've strayed so far from our beginnings. We've cut Mother Earth so deeply and in so many places. If we are going to heal ourselves, don't you think we should heal her first?"

He nodded, but he was quiet. We looked at each other for a long moment.

"Imagine what this was like," he said, gesturing to the concrete pillars outside, "before people got ahold of it?"

It was hard to imagine now, in this era of GMO foods and poisoned water systems, of natural disasters and man's unbridled destruction. We are so filled with our collective ego that we forget that we need the environment to stay alive. Humans can't create water, or gold, or oil, or animals. If we continue to ignore our responsibility to care for the soil, water, skies, and land, we will be the cause of our own extinction.

We are lost, scared of changing, learning, or growing. We are rigid in our assertion that our way is the right way. But when something isn't flexible, it breaks. And we are breaking— breaking our family life, breaking our health, breaking our desire to learn, breaking our economy, breaking our hearts and spirit.

There is no one to blame but ourselves, but it doesn't have to determine our future. We can choose to act differently. We can't play the same role. We must break our habits, our vices, and stop turning away from the terrible truths we have been ignoring for so long. We have to go without the gluttony and instead go forward, knowing that our silence is the same as our complicity.

A new hole burned into the sky. A new hole burned into our collective consciousness, into the very beat of our society's heart. The towers stood as a symbol of our country's exaltation of the all-mighty dollar, a token of our dominance and superiority. In my own life, the life I had built with such intention, the job that I loved that had helped to shape my identity, the very ground on which I stood and the very future in which I so fiercely believed—all were gone, all completely destroyed.

And now that it had been reduced to rubble, only questions remained in its stead. Where does the power go? What do we have faith in now, after the fall? How long will we keep building things, conquering land and people and resources, to prove our own worth to the world? What do I believe in now?

The breath caught in my throat, and the panic started to rise, creeping up from within me. My lungs struggled to find enough oxygen. *Inout, inout, inout.*

And then a now-familiar weight fell on my shoulder.

"Breathe," said Anthony softly beside me, his hand steady and sure. "Just breathe."

6

Heaven and Earth Collide

"What is happening out there?" asked Anthony.

"It's chaos," I said, but in my heart, I heard different words: *War. Conflict. Attack.*

We were being conquered.

The empire was falling. The battle had begun. The United States' long-standing reign felt as shaky as the floor beneath my feet in the tower. Our country was being challenged, and a chapter of absolute power was coming to a close.

Conquer. The word rang through my mind so clearly and resonated deep within me. It was an active word, one rooted in fear, one felt by so many of my ancestors before me as their homes and lives were laid to ruin by those who felt they should live, worship, behave differently. I felt their fear. I knew their pain.

That is what it felt like, that our rule was being usurped, that we were being overtaken, just like so many others had throughout all of history and modern mankind. I remembered, all at once. I remembered how my indigenous ancestors had been slain by the Spanish in the name of expansion. I could feel my memory of reading that my Native American and African ancestors had been forced out of their homes and into chains by the white side of the world and my family tree.

It was a generational ache that bloomed in my chest, a deep-seated trauma I'd inherited in my genetic code—one snippet of helix reserved for the map of my eyes, which shone bright like my father. One was for my curly brown hair, which looked just like my mom's. Another section held the memory of suffering, the dots and dashes of trauma from long ago.

Colonialism is a truly dirty word whose ash never seems to wash away. The forceful transfer of power never provides a clean break because the country that takes control can never fully develop when it holds people under its thumb. When resources are exploited, not shared, when citizens remain shackled because of their skin or by law, progress is slow real possibility.

Is this how my Ecuadorian ancestors felt when Tahuantinsuyu, the 1400s Incan stronghold, fell to ruins? When the Spanish invaded that shining Quitu-Cara capital, and rather than see their city conquered, the inhabitants burned it to the ground?

Whoever flew those planes had picked the towers for a reason—to attack the epicenter of power and prestige, to target the tallest buildings in the Western hemisphere, symbols and strongholds of wealth.

But they stole more than that, ruined more than that. The structures themselves had fallen, revealing a vulnerability our city and nation didn't know or believe existed. Our financial structure had stalled, choking on the ash that caked the streets. I wept for the people who had lost their lives as sacrifices to an unshared agenda, martyrs for a cause they hadn't signed up for. The despair I felt was total. The betrayal I felt was complete.

As a woman of color, I had known slivers of it before. I had spent my life trying to realize my democratic power in this country, constantly fighting for economic prosperity, having just cracked through the whitest, most male, oldest marketplace in the world. In that pursuit, the most frequent signposts were domination, injustice, and hypocrisy. They showed themselves in blatant and subtle forms: assumptions, sideways glances, or outright discrimination.

Feelings of sadness derived from injustice weren't new to me, but I had always been buoyed up by the reminder of what I had been fighting for: the chance to find my place and to carve out my own path. I had always longed not only to realize my dreams but also my own agency and power. Now, I was realizing those were gone, too.

I had been so privileged to have been able to sit at a desk in a Wall Street office, an opportunity that many of my black and brown sisters and brothers had never had. I had never taken it for granted, but the height of my historic gratitude now only deepened my grief. All of it had been destroyed. My place, my accomplishments, my purpose for waking up in the morning, the place I spent most hours of my days and life— nothing was left.

It came in waves, invaded my body in gulps and gasps, overwhelming and underscoring every breath. I felt history wash over me in ripples, like a tide, feelings of ancestral pain overlaid with acute trauma. I had been *that* close to it. I was on the front of this attack, at the center of this newly minted Wall Street war. Fear enveloped me, and with my head in my hands, flashes of ancestral memory, of the backstory of terrorism in this country, flitted across my mind.

Blood had been spilt on the ground beneath us centuries before, way before there was a New York City. The harbor had been surrounded by lush green, fed by the Hudson and East Rivers. Scholars have estimated that there may have been about 15,000 Lenape, the indigenous people of the northeastern woodlands, when the Europeans arrived and the Dutch tried to impose sovereignty over their culture, their lives. When the settlers arrived in 1524, the Lenape paddled canoes out into the harbor to meet Giovanni da Verrazano, the first European explorer to enter New York harbor, as he sailed in to claim their land as his own. One hundred and nineteen years later, the Lenape were systematically slaughtered in order to ensure Western dominance. Colonialism is the foundation of New York City.

I carry in my blood the spirit of my own Native ancestors. I was raised to know my culture, how I was Native American and African from my mom's side (Ortiz) and European and Native American from my dad's side (Quintero). At home, we spoke Spanish, and the world called us Hispanic or Latino, but I was Ecuadorian American. And yet, for years, I struggled with my identity because I never fit into a predefined label well enough to wear it fully. I wasn't really Latino because I couldn't speak Spanish with a nice flow and without an American accent, but I was too brown to just be American.

It wasn't until I was in college that I learned the true history of my people. I was enrolled in Seattle Central Community College, and my professor was my uncle, who had a PhD in Spanish language and literature.

"*Bienvenido*! Welcome to your first day of Latino American Colonial Literature. I applaud you all for wanting to learn about the Native lands, the Mexican lands we are on. Yes, Washington actually used to be Mexico!" he began.

He showed us the first maps of the Strait of Juan de Fuca, the passageway to the Pacific Northwest. These islands have Latino names, like the San Juan Islands, Lopez Island, and so when we study Latino history and literature, we're really learning of the first colonists and first peoples on this land which is American history. Whether in the northwest of South America or the northwest of North America, my European ancestors were among the first to colonize these lands.

"This class will look at the history and literature of Latino America for the past five centuries," my professor said to the class. "We will be studying pieces from Galeano, Todorov, and Weatherford. This class will give you a foundation of critical language and cultural skills to understand Latino American roots and the diversity of its identity, concepts that are not so easily understood by those in North America."

I beamed with pride seeing my Tio David in front of a room full of students, teaching, making jokes and truly waking everyone up with his passion. I think the piece that stuck with me the most was the excerpt from Todorov: *A young Indian woman of lovely and gracious appearance. She had promised her husband, fearful lest they should kill him in the war, not to have relations with any other man but him, and so no persuasion was sufficient to prevent her from taking her own life to avoid being defiled by another man; and because of this they had her thrown to the dogs.*

When I first read this, my belly churned. I could feel my face go red-hot like a tomato, I could feel the bile rising up in my throat. It made me disgusted that my European ancestors could do this to my Native and African ancestors. That young woman, that lovely and gracious woman with a non-white appearance who was thrown to the dogs, was not alone in her fate. Decades of European colonization in the Americas proved to be one of mankind's greatest holocausts. In central Mexico, according to one estimate, the indigenous population declined by about 85 percent in the century after the military conquest. Other estimates put that number even higher, I seem to recall a number maybe closer to 95 percent.

That history was studded by cruelty. For example, Alonso de Zorita, who valued plants more than human life, famously said, "If it doesn't rain, the plants will get watered by the blood of Natives." The one I hated the most, the one I couldn't read anymore, was Diego de Landa, who stabbed children's bellies because they couldn't walk as fast as their mothers. Or the famous Vasco Nunez de Balboa, who would butcher Native elders, children, women, and men, just to test out the sharpness of his blade.

And now, there were thousands burned, thousands squashed, thousands obliterated. Not by a sword, not devoured by dogs, nor raped before their deaths, but nevertheless heartlessly taken from us all, just for being alive, just for going to work, just for being in a building that symbolized all the things others choose to hate.

It was part of a colonialist cycle that has played out again and again throughout history. I was a college student when California's Proposition 187 passed, the modern version of colonial suppression. The law took away public services from people without documentation, as though papers were more important than the people who held them. What was so clear to me was that this law attacking immigrants was beyond ironic—these immigrants were the original inhabitants of California.

I was a sophomore at Seattle Central Community College and the President of the Association of Latino American Students when the "English Only" movement was gaining steam and Proposition 187 singled out Mexican immigrants—the farmers, the landscapers, the cleaners, the nannies, the cooks, and so many more. Though it was immigration-based, in truth, it was only a thin veil for racial discrimination. By profiling brown people, it reinforced and reinvigorated the age-old concept that America is for whites only.

As a student leader, terrified that similar laws would be passed in my state, I planned a protest caravan to go to Olympia, Washington. When the day came, it was rainy, but we were determined. We protested outside with bullhorns and posters, then we went inside the main chamber, where we were met with fear. "Please don't break anything," the man at the door said, recoiling at the sight of this group of brown-skinned students fighting for what we believed in. I could tell he was worried that he had let us in. The lawmakers weren't in the house, so we began thinking of our next move.

What I couldn't stand being confronted with was reading Todorov's *The Conquest of America* and how the Native people of that land who were entrusted with peace were the same people being persecuted today. Those who had held onto the ability to keep their culture through the treaty of Guadalupe just 150 years ago were being systematically attacked by Proposition 187.

It was like seeing the hate of the white settlers all over again, only this time through their children and grandchildren as if both ancestors and descendants had united to keep us oppressed for another 500 years. A good example was the day laborers being paid in cash at the same time as they were economically oppressed—their labor was welcome but not their lives or their children's lives.

Another example was the removal of language from culture. Years and years after Mexicans were forced to abandon their indigenous language in favor of their Spanish oppressors', they were once again being forced to change to whatever the dominant culture dictated. Spanish is, in fact, a colonial language, but it was no longer the favored language of the oppressors, the supporters of Proposition 187. The truth was, we had been colonized twice over—first by the Spanish, second by the white man. The Unz movement or the English only campaign; it was always about how far they could contort brown peoples lives, values, lands, and bodies to match what those in power demanded.

"Anthony, are you Catholic?" I asked, my mind coming back to the present.

"Where did that come from?" he asked with a hint of amusement at my non sequitur.

"Well, you look Italian, and your name, Anthony, is a very Catholic name."

"Yeah, I'm Catholic," he said after a few seconds. "Named after St. Anthony, the saint of lost and stolen things. But to be honest, I am not a practicing Catholic. I've been so focused on work that I haven't really spent much time in the church."

"Maybe that's a good thing," I said, not because I was against faith or religion. But because I knew the history of this country, that its founders and the wars they waged to forcibly make the land and people their own was often justified by, or because of, religion.

I first learned that in class, but I studied it later in college and in the years following, so deep was the root that the truth had planted in me. "The Age of Discovery," those missions to find new worlds, was fueled by the belief and obligation of propagating the Catholic faith. "The Age of Discovery" was an almost laughable misnomer—indigenous people weren't discovered. They were slaughtered.

In the 1400s, Pope Alexander VI, who was a Spaniard, explicitly endorsed his home country's right to implement Christianity throughout the world, which then became Spain's singular focus in the years to come. Ordained with Church-bestowed power and purse strings, the Spanish pursued three goals: "conquer, convert, and become rich."

And so they invaded, taking to the seas to push outward and put the people they met underneath their rule and their laws. They were rivaled by Portugal, which was also a powerhouse of expansion, and in tandem, they took over each land where their boats met the shore. They set sail across the Atlantic, the Indian, and the Pacific Oceans. I remember reading how in the late 1400s, Pope Alexander VI issued a missive, the

Treaty of Tordesillas, dividing these newly conquered lands along a pole-to-pole line through the Atlantic to split the trade, riches, lands, and people between the Spanish and Portuguese. They hadn't even traveled and seen the Americas, they were still thinking these were islands, calling them the West Indies.

If explorers found cities, they claimed them, murdering the leaders, taking the riches, dismantling the culture, spreading disease, and subjugating the people. The initial waves of violence were followed by more insidious treatment of those left behind—the conquerors enforced their belief in the Catholic faith, stripping people of their customs and ceremonies and creating a reliance on the Roman Catholic church. In the name of saving these people's souls, they destroyed their lives.

The history of dominance is deep. Constantine I, the Roman emperor from 306 to 337, was the first emperor in history to convert to Christianity. Under his rule, he altered one of the 10 commandments by changing the day of rest, the Sabbath, from the seventh to the first day of the week. He decreed that all the spirits and energies of localized religions were actually Satan's influence (a personification of spirits) and stripped people of their right to practice ritual and ceremony with the energies and spirits of the Earth. He took everyone off the lunar calendar, which was rooted in nature's cycles, and created the Gregorian calendar. His religion, his skin, his European blood, his dominant culture became the driving force to conquer the rest of the world. European tribes fell in line, lost their own culture, and sought the protection of the Roman Catholic church, a religious-political powerhouse that felt it was their own divine right to brutalize and terrorize people of color around the world and dominate.

It always stuck with me, what Desmond Tutu said, how they only wanted the lands and gold from them. We were the heathens, the ones who needed saving, yet all the terror came from them. They gave us the

Bible and took our lands. Now we clench to the Bible and have no place to call home.

These dynamics—light-skinned men asserting dominance over brown-skinned people—are the foundations of modern-day white supremacy—a supremacy rooted in the genocide of Native peoples, equating black lives as property to build wealth, and the maintenance of a forever war with foreigners. In the 1400s and 1500s, Europeans were the most powerful people on the planet. The conquistadors who committed unspeakable acts, who committed all manner of sin, were told it was their right and obligation to impose their will and beliefs upon indigenous people. Their church, their God, had deemed it so. Their purity and power were ordained. Their culture was superior. Their religion was irrefutable. Their whiteness was one of their most powerful weapons of all—terrorizing and brutalizing people of color all around the world wasn't just an option, it was their divine responsibility.

And what a huge burden that placed on the oppressed. To lessen the brutality, be the good Indian, kill your ancestral religion, and convert. Speak our language. Take on our culture.

"Why do we keep doing this to each other?" I asked Anthony.

"Doing what?"

"Killing. Murdering. Destroying everything. And in the name of what? Power? Politics?"

"Some people are just crazy, I think," he said, and there was sadness in his voice. "Seems to me that some people just have so much fear and hate in them, they have to put it somewhere."

I felt so defeated, holding this sinful history in my mind right next to a memory of trauma so fresh I could still smell the scalded metal on my skin. The colonials plundered everything, obliterated communities and lives and the foundation of an entire continent. And now, the Big Apple, the lushest fruit born of that historic destruction, was being attacked?

Time would tell if we would fall, but the city was burning and bloodied, and the souls of thousands hung in the ashen air all around us. Whatever the men who flew the planes hated, I was a part of it. Whatever they were fighting for or against, in their eyes, I was the enemy.

But in so many ways, I was just like them, frustrated with a system designed to oppress, cast off by colonialism and capitalism that cared more for wealth and power than human beings, misrepresented by leaders who saw lives as currency.

My own parents left Ecuador because there was no middle class, no clear way to grow economically. It was a cash crop economy, one that benefited a handful of wealthy families and was driven by Western demand for particular natural resources. Coffee, chocolate, and bananas are what Ecuador was known for, a constant give with very little return. We gave all our wealth, all the benefits of our land, and our lives.

By the time my parents left Ecuador in the 1960s, colonialism had been transformed into a sophisticated technological global system that included marketplaces, currencies, debt, and government subsidies promoting the west that were based in the west. The buying and trading of natural resources from around the world still relied on the labor of the poor, and the margins were still not equitably invested in the places where the natural resources were grown and harvested. It was a continuation of the economic injustice that began with the European colonists and was backed by the church.

I learned how the world worked at a very young age. My dad Ruben, who was the oldest, would sit around with his brothers: Tio David, the professor, Tio Cesar, the youngest of all the siblings on my dad's side, and Tio Arturo, my mom's younger brother, also a PhD candidate. My brother Paul often joined them, and because TV was boring, and I didn't really care for what the women would speak of, I'd just listen and hang out with the men.

I can recall one moment in particular as a little girl in the 1980s. Tio Arturo lived in a house on Eastlake outside of Seattle that had multiple floors overlooking Lake Union. He was known on campus and in the city for having the best parties. We felt as if we brought salsa to Seattle as we always had the best music, and the parties were the only place to get *sancocho*. After the music and the food faded away in the wee morning hours, the intellectual, political conversations would begin. One morning in the 1980's I remember being around the table with only men.

They'd talk about the beauty of Ecuador, but then they'd quickly start speaking about El Salvador, Guatemala, and Nicaragua. All of these Latino American countries were experiencing similar circumstances—civil unrest, killings, people having to flee their native lands. The news was blaring the Iran Contra scandal, and there were rumblings about cocaine, guns, revolutions, and the sought-after canal in Nicaragua that never happened because the people wouldn't allow it.

"The Sandinistas have been fighting for centuries," said Tio Cesar. "The powers that be want a canal there and are determined to build it."

"Yes, and the colonists have now created economic imperialism, which has continuously obliterated Central American democracies," countered Tio Arturo. "The families in power have been bribed to apply for bank loans, and then once the multinational corporations see a movement for labor unions, they pull out all investments and leave the country *plantado* [left with nothing]."

"The worst thing, though, is that it's no longer sugar, coffee, and bananas running the show," said my father knowingly.

"Yeah, the white God is now cocaine!" said Tio's friend.

"The cash crops keep changing and keep bringing profits for the middlemen and those who run the supply chain. The guns, the cocaine, the devastation—all fueled by violence, all to build power for those who already have it," said Tio Cesar.

"It's the colonialist cycle—destroy the culture, take over the control, enslave the people, maintain the power at all costs," said my father. "But the people almost always rise up."

Back in the cab, all I could think about was wondering if the attackers had dealt with this type of economic dynamic, they must have seen their loved ones suffer. Why else would they have done what they did?

Even though the terror of colonialism had ended, the customs of cultural dominance through the physical evolution of our global economy just complicate the economic injustice that occurs around the world.

No reparations have ever cured or settled the harm done. The creation of corporations just veiled and protected the leaders with a corporate body. For instance, in Ecuador, the United Fruit Company enjoyed unprecedented economic and political power in the region in the early to mid-1900s. After the collapse of the cocoa bean industry in the 1920s, the United Fruit Company, now the parent company of Chiquita Banana, moved into the region by purchasing a resource-rich plantation in Tenguel. They recruited workers who were happy to join—the pay was steady and came with benefits like company-sponsored housing, stores, and a soccer club. Even the labor union was actually shadow sponsored by the company itself. There were no jobs for women, only men, but the company paid the men so well that the women weren't disappointed by the lack of income opportunities for them.

Supported by government infrastructure, which would, in turn, benefit financially from the company's presence in the country, business boomed. At one point, Ecuador produced more than 25% of the world's bananas.

But what was at times an idyllic setup became a corporate nightmare in the 1960s after the banana crop was decimated by disease. The company was forced to cut back, firing people in droves, which meant they not only lost their jobs they also lost their homes. People were hopeless, and the company they had relied on had no solutions to offer, so they gathered together. On March 27, 1962, the workers invaded Tenguel and seized the land. What followed was a decades-long battle for power and control, although the heart of the issue was simple: on one side was corporate colonialism, and on the other was the people who had historic claim to the land and needed to reclaim it to grow food and feed their families. It was the exact cycle my father had said, and he was right. Just as my ancient ancestors had burned their capital instead of seeing it taken over by European invaders, the Ecuadorian people rose up.

And this wasn't the last time. I remember hearing that the same company wreaked havoc on Nicaragua in the 1980s. Tia Elide's father fought for the Sandinistas when he was just a teenager. From Honduras, he went to Nicaragua to fight with them for sovereignty when he was in his mid-20s. He battled for the basics of human necessity: access to water, land to raise a family, resources to grow food, the right to retain cultural identity. What was often deemed and disguised as communism was, in fact, just the pursuit of human survival. The taxonomy, the labels of political entities, did not distract from the real, deep need for people to have access to their homes, their historic place on the planet. Tia Elide's father lived, but so many did not. And what for? For money? For power? At what price and for what ultimate purpose?

"Why did they attack us?" I asked Anthony back in the cab, still stuck on that one essential question. Though I didn't know which men were flying those planes, all I could think was that it felt like a modern rebellion, their own uprising against whatever struggle they had been forced into.

"It must be so bad where they are living, so terrible for their loved ones," I continued. "They and everyone they love must have no future and be living in hell to kill themselves to kill us. Death must be the only way to make a point or to have freedom. What else could explain it?"

Anthony didn't answer me, but his brow was furrowed, and his head shook from side to side. Perhaps there were no answers to the questions I had. Could we, as mere civilians, be just like them? Or be blamed for what our leaders do? For this capitalist framework that we have created and maintained? Could this be some crazy and radical way for them to do something to wake us up? I kept trying to understand the injustice, but the price of rebellion was so many lives lost.

Maybe those who attacked us were going through this, though? Maybe they had no power? Maybe they had no future? Maybe they were trying to call out to us to wake us up to their reality? Maybe their leaders weren't listening, and they needed a way to get their attention? There were so many unknowns, and in the absence of fact, as I often did, I looked to faith. I remembered Matthew 5:44: *Love your enemies, bless them that curse you, do good to them that hate you, and pray for them which despitefully use you, and persecute you.*

7

My Brother's Keeper

We turned left on Park Avenue, and it hit me that within a few blocks, we'd be at Grand Central Station. Having never had a car in the city, I hadn't internalized the surface roads in the same way I knew the subway by heart. All I could imagine was a plane, missile, bomb, or some other disaster bursting through Grand Central's roof and breaking the celestial golden ceiling into rubble. I could feel the panic rise in my throat. It tasted like bile, thick and impossible to choke down.

"What are you doing!?" I yelled at the taxi driver, leaning between the front seats.

"Ma'am, I'm just driving up to the East Side, as we discussed."

"No, no, no," I moaned. "You can't take us near Grand Central. If they could destroy the towers, what's to say they won't hit here next? There are so many people here… it's the perfect target!"

I put my head in my hands, rocking back and forth, the idea of that celebrated building collapsing seeming like an inevitability.

"Ma'am, it's okay. This is the most direct way," the driver said.

We were already looping around the station, the antique green finish a blur from my window. I felt nauseous, the car sickness I got as a little girl coming back. I looked next to me at Anthony—his face was red, sweat beading on his brow.

"It's okay," he said, though I could see the nervousness in his eyes. "We'll be fine. We won't be here that long."

Our eyes met. "Breathe, right? Just like before. Just focus on your breath."

I did as he said, and I felt myself getting calmer with each exhale. But still, the anxiety and the nausea knocked at me from the inside. I scooted over next to the door and put my elbow on the windowsill, covering my whole mouth with my hands. Looking out, my gut rose up, and I realized that it was almost lunchtime, but I hadn't eaten anything. My bagel and coffee were back on my desk at work, covered in ash, waiting for me. I felt a squeeze of my throat as I exhaled, trying to push the image and anxiety out, but it just kept going further and further upward until it passed my heart and reached my throat. I kept my hands over my face, gripping my mouth like a vice. Were there bombs in the air? What was flying in the sky above us? I prayed. *Please, God, let us pass. Please, God, keep us safe.*

We reached a light, facing North on Park, at the northern entrance to the station, and when the light turned green, I relaxed as we crawled away. I could breathe deeper. I felt instantaneously calmer leaving that landmark behind.

"You see," said Anthony. "Everything worked out."

"Thank God," I said, but now that I had unclenched, the words were ready to fly out. "But that was just by chance. As we saw today, we can't count on the authorities or the government or the United States military to protect us. We've got the best armed forces in the entire world, two people for each position even, the biggest budget on planet

Earth, and still they can't keep our own commercial planes from nose-diving into our buildings. We're like sitting ducks in this city."

Though my fear was still there, suddenly I was so angry. So many people had died, and so many weren't even warned about what was happening. There was no announcement in the towers themselves. So many floors I passed didn't even have fire alarms. Whoever was supposed to be protecting us, whatever systems had been designed to keep us safe, they had failed. So many people had died.

It felt like such an injustice that I found myself asking, "Do they really care?" The images of all those people, singed and drenched and crammed into the stairwell like cattle, clambering to get out alive—it was all I saw when I closed my eyes.

When I opened them, I saw a sign that I had walked past hundreds of times—the buffed-stone-embossed logo for JPMorgan Chase Bank. All that wealth amassed in this country for hundreds of years... and as I looked down at my arm, at the brown skin I was born with, I couldn't help but wonder: What had all that money been built on?

I retreated to memory again, sitting in class at Blanchet High School in Mr. Wilkinson's class. He taught history, with a focus that year on minority studies. It was an interesting area of expertise for a tall, blue-eyed veteran with blondish white hair who had served in combat, but with a strong voice and powerful presence, he was fully capable of corralling a room of unruly teenagers. He commanded respect, and we all gave it to him.

But right then, in the cab, I remembered so clearly the lessons that he taught us and the heartache that followed and stayed with me ever since. He was the first teacher I'd ever had who actually shared what was happening to people of color, who cared enough to place a lens on our collective history.

He told us how the big banks—JPMorgan, Citizens Bank, Bank of America, and Wells Fargo—all benefited from the slave trade. The commodities needed to fuel the mid-1800s American economy, to further this country's illustrious progress, were built on the backs of African Americans. The cotton they picked accounted for more than half of overseas shipments, and what wasn't sold to foreign buyers was shipped to be milled in the northeast. The money that traded hands was stored, accrued, and siphoned out of their accounts.

And if ever a plantation owner needed a loan, the ownership of people was one of the most accepted forms of collateral. If a plantation owner defaulted on his loan payments, banks took ownership of the people who were propertized, and they would then be bought and sold to fuel other transactions and strengthen the bank's margins. To know I worked on Wall Street, to be reminded that even New York City, the most beautiful, gleaming, vibrant city on Earth, benefited from slavery was its own tragedy. A testament to the direct fiscal connection between the sale of human lives and today's economy: the stock market is only 500 feet away from where the city's enslavement market used to be.

This union, its founders and leaders, had taken so much from my Native and African American ancestors—land, culture, health, language, connection to the Earth, independence, and so much more.

Old memories continued to play through my mind. Driving by those Midtown banks on the day our country had been so brutally attacked triggered an incredible response in me, unearthing all the lessons I had learned about our nation's founding and place in the world.

In college, in search of my own Latina identity, I studied African American history specifically and learned more about the leaders during the Civil War and the 13th Amendment, another layer of our past. I remembered learning about the many African American politicians who exercised their agency, used their voices, and had the votes to win elections and gain real power. It was the first time I had ever learned that Charles Sumner truly grasped the political movement of freedom and about the first national civil rights bill to ban discrimination and segregation in schools, churches, and public spaces. They were the change-makers, the transformative leaders who had pushed the 14th and 15th Amendments to go beyond the fold.

Then to learn of the dark abyss, the political blasphemy that violated the gospel of liberty. How the conservative President Johnson organized a "lily-white government with blatant proslavery biases and appointed Governors in 1865 and 1866 to enact the Black Codes throughout intended to reestablish slavery under another name." This, coupled with the creation of the KKK, a paramilitary organization whose job was to use violence with stealth, murder, economic intimidation, and political assassinations by the political use of terror, made me physically ill.

It sickened me then, when I had first learned it, and every day since. As I sat in the back of the cab, I couldn't get past thinking of the sins of our country, our leaders, and our culture. I thought of all we had done wrong, all the hatred we had put out into the world. And I realized: this is our reckoning. All the seeds of terror we had sewn for generations had finally resulted in this.

Collectively, we had always placed possessions over people. I could see why Jesus said in Mark 10:25: *It is easier for a camel to go through the eye of a needle, than for a rich man to enter into the kingdom of God.* It's not the riches that make evil; it's what people do with those riches and whether one is able to relinquish the oppressive mindset that accompanies generational wealth. Though it is undoubtedly the right thing to do, it is simply not a personally profitable exercise to face, reconcile, or rectify historical sins.

That's how we got here, I thought.

"Is it okay if we take a quick break?" asked the taxi driver, jarring me from the depth of my thoughts. "I need to stop and get something to drink. Is that okay?"

Where are we? I wondered, looking around outside to see the state of things. Was it chaos, or was it peaceful?

"Yes, of course," Anthony replied. "We've been in here for hours. It would be nice to stand up for a bit."

The taxi driver pulled over to the right, stopping just in front of a bodega.

Anthony asked me, "Do you want anything? You want to get outside for a bit?"

"No, thank you, I'd rather stay put, thanks." I felt safe in the cab, a yellow checkered cocoon in the face of all the change outside.

But after they left, the familiar panic started to rise, my lungs suddenly struggling to find air again. I opened the door and stood just outside, stretching slightly, trying to will the numbness out of my muscles and mind. I noticed a man on the sidewalk approaching me, his mouth open, his eyes hungry. I looked the other way as he smacked his lips and stared.

"You're beautiful, *mami*. Looking so hot, I just want to take you home with me!"

Like a whip, my core filled with fire, my mind a white-hot inferno, my words lashing out at him.

"How *dare* you try to come on to me right now! Don't you understand what is happening in the world? We just got attacked! People died in those towers, and you're speaking to me with no respect for what we lost today? What is your problem? Even during war, all you can think about is pussy!?"

His eyes grew with every word I hurled at him. Everyone on the street stopped and stared. It felt like the whole city had gotten quiet. He shook his head and waved his hands, his entire tone shifting under the weight and shock of what I said.

"Ma'am, I truly apologize. I am so sorry. I didn't mean anything by it." His cheeks reddened, and he backed up, shuffling off to wherever he came from as quickly as he could.

I couldn't hold back the tears. The trauma I had experienced, the grief that still hadn't settled, the shock that infiltrated every pore—that mattered. But more than anything, I realized I had forgotten. Even during war, perhaps particularly during war, I could be a target, that women are always targets for opportunistic men who feel empowered to attack. I went back inside the cab.

Women are almost always among the ranks of casualty, either by bodily violation or body count, and I wasn't safe during this day of war. Terror has always been part of the American experience.

The cab was quiet. The sun shone down on the Upper East Side, making the concrete sparkle and sway. I breathed deeply. All the way uptown, I could barely smell the smoke, though I carried it with me, infused into each strand of hair.

"It's time to go," I heard a soft voice say. "Are you sure you don't want anything?"

"No, thank you," I replied, looking up to see Anthony and the taxi driver. "I'm fine."

Seeing their faces, I truly did feel fine. My body relaxed with relief at seeing these two good men who had treated me with respect and each other so kindly on this day.

They got back into the cab, and soon those same words left Anthony again—*it's time to go*. We were only a few blocks away from where he needed to be.

"There's a lot of traffic, it looks like. You can just bring me to the corner, and you guys can keep going." He intended to get out at 59th and 3rd to cross the Queensboro Bridge and make it back to his place in Queens. "The lights are gree,n so I'll jump out quickly."

The cab driver pulled over.

"This is good, sir. Thank you so much."

"Here," he said to me, pressing a small fold of bills into my hand. "This is all I got, but I hope that it helps you."

"Thank you so much, Anthony!" My hand found his. I struggled to find the words to thank him, to mark what we had shared. "Thank you for sharing the cab with me and just being here for me."

He smiled, and I realized it was the first time I had seen his face take that shape. He had a brightness about him. Even on this dark day, his light shone through.

"You take care, get home and call your mom as soon as you can," he said.

He opened the door and stepped out onto the sidewalk. He was a stranger, but his generosity was a gift and his spirit a salve to the wounds of that day. We had shared so much kindness, and he had created space for me to process this grief, giving me everything he had, even though he still had miles to go before he arrived back at his home. In the midst of his own trauma, his own shock and grief, he had shown me such kindness and compassion.

It was hard to rectify the connection we shared with the thoughts still parading through my mind. This white man had just shown me, a person of color, incredible humanity. And yet other white men throughout history were capable of causing immense pain.

Inching along in the heavy traffic, I felt the trauma our oppressed brothers and sisters had lived through, the lives our Black and brown city kids were born into. As we drove up 3rd Avenue and into Harlem, we made a left on 125th, but the traffic was thick, so we went up Park Avenue and turned west again. As the cab was turning right on Lenox, I saw two young teenagers, one a tall, slender brother and the other an outgoing, filled-out one, rockin' a natural. They were hanging, talking, and chilling on the corner. My window was down, and I was just looking at the people and the neighborhood, stuck in my own mind, as though I was watching a movie. My body was limp and lifeless from exhaustion. I felt almost invisible until the big, boisterous brother looked at me.

He looked me directly in the eye and said to me, "You were there?!? Weren't you?!?" I tried to say yes, but I had been silent for so long that my throat felt dry, almost closed together—still, I managed to nod.

He smiled, a "wow" forming on his lips. He and his friend jumped up and down like they had met a celebrity, breaking into a celebratory dance on the sidewalk. Though the unnatural clouds still seared the sky, I thought perhaps I was as close as they had gotten to a day that would go down in history.

"Ohhhh!!!" he yelled, slapping his friend's hand. "Can you believe I called it?? It's Armageddon!"

The light changed. They hopped off the corner and crossed the street behind me, yelling as they went. *It's the end of the world!*

We kept driving north on Lenox a few blocks, and when we stopped at 135th Street, I could see the Schomburg Center for Research in Black Culture, named in honor of Señor Arturo Alfonso Schomburg, an Afro-Borinqueño born in Santurce, Puerto Rico. The building was dedicated to collecting, preserving, and providing free access to the documented history of Black life in America and around the world. And as an activist, writer, and historian, he ensured that all history and literature of people of African descent would live on. I could imagine the obstacles he faced in pursuit of his passion.

I felt a kinship with him and his calling. My own African lineage comes mostly from my mother and her Afro-Latino great-grandmother,

Rupertina Ayarza-Herrera. Her grandfather was a general under Bolivar who was honored for protecting Guayaquil independence time and time again. He was actually from Panama, his name was Fernando Ayarza, and he eventually became a colonel. Family history tells stories of a zealous leader, Garcia Moreno, who had our beloved colonel, my ancestor, imprisoned in his golden years. He was flogged naked and buried inside a dungeon despite countless attempts from outside politicians and leaders to set him free. It was one of many such stories in Ecuadorian history—Afro-Ecuadorians were still strongly discriminated against.

In so many ways, I knew I had no reason to truly be upset about my own station and situation in life. I was light-skinned and working in one of the most powerful industries on the globe. But I felt the collective injustice of my ancestors deep in my bones. The pain, the dominance of economic might, the abuse of power and privilege centuries-old.

Looking out my window and driving up Audubon, I could see the people, the children, and even with so much strife, the city's children reminded me of the history in this neighborhood. The Harlem Renaissance and the forgotten generations of kids who had come afterward. The kids who slipped through the cracks of drugs, prisons, and economic deprivation. The kids who weren't ever set up to succeed. The kids who were systematically beaten and broken down to ensure they would stay forgotten.

Those same children who society cast off created something beautiful and transformative out of that suffering, the birth of hip hop. They had created the only unrecognized contemporary art movement in the US, which has expanded worldwide. Their art, culture, music, and existence raised in the forgotten boroughs of our minds, with all its inequities, with its injustice, became the opposite of what its oppressors had intended—they inspired the whole world. It was a world of four elements: breaking, writing/graffiti, emceeing, and deejaying. I explored the culture through dancing, my chosen form of expression, one that I was told was a sin by my religion but one that taught me the true meaning of unconditional love and healing. Hip hop came into my life in the 1980s through the radio, my older siblings, the television watching the Rock Steady Crew and New York City Breakers on TV. Music was always playing in my home, whether it was salsa, classical, jazz, the blues, boleros, or rock. Even as a child in elementary school, the music made me feel so alive!

I remember seeing the first b-boy crew perform for a presidential inauguration, President Regan's inauguration, to be exact, on TV in my living room, where I watched it as a starry-eyed kid. Now I literally lived blocks away from Lil Lep, one of the stars of that performance, a true hip-hop architect who was now a dear friend.

Lep and Fever were as close as they come, knit together through friendship and hardship. They were a family, them and the other b-boys from around the city and around the world, a network of strength, creativity, and support. At first, I thought it was a b-boy thing, that creating and dancing together brought people closer. But the truth was that it was a necessity. It was hard to live. It was hard to survive. It was hard to escape a society, a city, that was not designed to keep people growing and thriving.

Lep would always remind me that hip hop was born in the Bronx, just like him, and that the Bronx of his childhood was always burning. The neighborhood, once predominantly Italian and Jewish communities, had evolved over the years. By the 1970s, they were mostly filled with African American residents and immigrants of color. It was then that the Bronx started burning.

In the late 1970s, fires tore through that borough: seven neighborhoods lost 97 percent of their buildings, and 44 lost more than

50 percent. While it was long speculated that these fires were sparked by arson—angry tenants torching their own buildings—the truth was far more nefarious than that. Decades of lack of access to capital, pensions, or a fair wage, along with discriminatory practices and government policies that influenced how and where people lived, created systemic conditions of economic neglect that eventually led landlords to abandon and often burn their properties.

Neglect was often the spark of the fires—faulty wiring, space heaters, gas leaks, and other infrastructural problems paired with shoddy craftsmanship and flammable materials meant that in many ways, those buildings were built to burn. But when they wouldn't burn on their own, landlords sometimes took matters into their own hands. They were frequently given no-questions-asked insurance policies, which meant a burned building was often worth more than a standing one.

This situation was compounded by bureaucratic involvement—in the 1970s, the New York City Fire Department was told it had to help close the city's budget deficit and find a few million dollars. They proposed closing 13 of the city's fire stations, many of which were located in the smoldering South Bronx. And the city suffered from infrastructure problems of its own—it is estimated that up to a third of fire hydrants weren't functional.

Redlining, the post-Depression-era practice of denying financial, health and even supermarkets in neighborhoods that are predominantly communities of color, or as the market states, "deemed a financial risk". The Bronx might as well have had a solid red circle around it, designating all the areas where Black, Puerto Rican, and other people of color lived. Mortgage lenders used that demographic demarcation to designate an area as "high risk," which was then used to deny loans to people in those neighborhoods, effectively trapping them where they were. With no loans and access to health services, many had no choice but to accept the living conditions that had been built for them.

People of color are never seen, whether in school text books, society, or in history, but what leader in their right mind would allow blocks and blocks of the Bronx to be burned down and let families live through a war-torn zone without any government intervention or any aid to the area?

But those conditions were, as it turns out, the incubator of hip hop. Imagine being a teenager and coming home one day to see your home reduced to ash, left with nothing? Then imagine knowing it was almost a certainty that it would happen again. Your family members gone, losing what little they had, knowing that no one was coming to help them. It was a form of domestic terrorism. And those were only some of the stories I heard from Lil Lep and some of the other cultural architects, the founding fathers of the hip-hop movement.

They told me about their childhoods, stolen from them, robbed not only of innocence but of hope. With buildings burning, bricks in piles, garbage stacked up on the streets around them, and loss all around. But instead of lying down, instead of rolling over, instead of giving in, these children grew up to channel that strife, trauma and hardship into something creative. Graffiti was its own artform, modern-day hieroglyphics with a mission.

They didn't have instruments, but they could take two vinyl records, juggle the beat, and become a deejay. They could take that rhythmic prose and everything they had in their hearts and minds to become the master of ceremonies, to birth emceeing. Then came the dancers, with their mix of cultures, mixing the top rock with an aggressive energy that could take all their acrobatic, martial arts, disco, hustle, and mambo and turn it into breakdancing, giving life to b-boys and b-girls. It was contemporary tribal dance, an age-old practice of coming together and indulging in self-expression. Those dancers would use cut-up cardboard boxes or left-over linoleum tile from an abandoned lot and tape them down on the streets. It was easier to spin that way, but if they had to, they'd practice on the concrete.

It would have been so easy to focus on what they didn't have, on what they had lost, and I'm sure many did. But instead, they focused on their joy, their music, their dance, their art, their sounds with whatever they had around them, and that is what made the movement. That is what built a culture that helps the world spin to this day. It was a creative powerhouse, a masterful manipulation of cast-off materials and cast-off dreams, a way to transmute what they had been given into what they could imagine and find a way to take their imagination beyond their reality.

These were the forgotten children. The most powerful city in the United States, perhaps the world, didn't offer its aid. It did not respond when these families were screaming in agony that their lives were on fire, that their neighborhoods were falling apart all around them. But when these people realized that help was never going to come, they looked at the pain all around them and transformed it into power.

And just when they started to rise up with creativity, those who didn't understand their plight, decided that what they were doing should be outlawed. There should be no dancing in the streets, there should be no reclaiming of empty walls with cans of paint. The city would not offer itself as a canvas to these children. Instead, they would be deemed as criminals. The trauma of this period created the most beautiful contemporary art movement that is now the global hip-hop phenomena.

They were some of the original hip-hop artists, and they were not alone. Hip hop was born in this hardness, this systematic deprivation, this pain. And still, all its cultural architects overcame. Their hearts were hurt, but their skin was thick, and their creativity knew no bounds.

In the cab, I rolled the window down and rested my cheek on the sill, breathing in the smells and sounds of the city as these memories rolled over me, replacing some of my sadness about the pain of the past with a glimmer of hope for the future.

Living in New York, trying to get home to the boogie down where it all started, I understand the terms "gritty of the city" and "concrete jungle." The city was so diverse, with so many people from all walks of life, and the backdrop was hard rock, cement, concrete. The streets and the buildings were so old, thousands, possibly millions, must have walked on them and lived in them, and the people were so bright, so full of color, so full of character, music, and energy imbued by all that history.

So much of the past is so dark, and being in those buildings that morning, seeing New York burn once again, I had one resounding hope: that we could get back to us. That we could realize the pain that we as people and as a country have caused so many for so long. Maybe this is our shot, our chance to come together and truly have a reckoning so we can fix issues at the root. Can we take this time of loss and finally choose to make things right? Right now?

8

In the Flow

When death comes to you, you listen. When you stare finality in the face, it's your duty to pay attention to what is reflected back at you.

Many survivors of near-death experiences say your life flashes before your eyes, a rapid-fire movie of all your memories, all the moments and people that matter most to you in the years spent on this Earth. But mine was a collection of past experiences displayed, and a sensory journey, an exploration of my physical and spiritual selves. In many ways, it was an awakening.

In the cab, I rested my head against the window frame, looking out onto the city. We were driving through north Harlem on a windy road that ebbed and swayed, rolled and crested. At the top of each hill, it felt like we intertwined with the sky.

In my belly, a muffled *boom boom boom* in rhythm with my heart. It filled my ears but then would fade back to near silence, this metronome in my chest. Stress, I thought. Fear. Once I rested, it would go away. I was sure of it.

As we got closer to the Bronx, the traffic was locked into place. We inched down the road, and home felt painfully far away. I looked down at my clothes—the blouse I loved, now sooty and sweat-soaked; the slacks I had slapped on that morning, now stained with soot and smoke; the boots, scuffed and soaking wet. I tried to wipe away my tears, but just as I did, another one would follow. I didn't know I had that much sadness in me, waiting to come out.

Without my own St. Anthony, patron saint of lost things, to guide me and buoy me, I was bone-tired and anxious for even the smallest slice of peace. Home was the only place I could think to find it, but with all the destruction of the day, I was terrified there wasn't much left of it.

All of Manhattan was trying to get off the island to their own safe havens, or even just to put distance between them and the terror they had seen, felt, and smelled. To avoid the unknown terror to come. At this rate, it felt like it was going to take hours to get where we were going, so I took the time to do a check of my body—tired, yes. Sore, undoubtedly. But I felt a deep reservoir of energy in me still, my emergency supply, my dig deep reserve.

"Sir?' I asked the driver, whose eyes found me in the rear-view mirror. I felt like I would be able to recognize him anywhere, just from that swath of skin from his forehead to the bridge of his nose. "I think I can walk from here."

"Are you sure, ma'am?"

"I'm sure. My place isn't far, and you have been so kind. Thank you so much for getting us to where we need to go and for seeing this through."

He nodded his head, and though I expected to see relief in his reaction, instead, I saw concern.

"Will you go straight home?" he asked.

"I'll get home safe," I replied, touched at his compassion. "I don't have any cash on me, but here is the money that Anthony gave me. I'm sorry it's not more."

He accepted it and turned around in his seat for the first time to face my direction.

"I am happy you are safe," he said, and with great emphasis on each word, as though every syllable had its own gravity: "You take care of yourself."

"I will," I said, my voice wavering slightly, and opened the door.

I needed to cross the street. Though Broadway was normally a busy thoroughfare, not one car was driving into the city. I walked across the empty lane to the west side of the street and began to walk north.

My limbs responded happily to the motion, and I found my stride— walking, looking, feeling, noticing the green of the trees, the thick cobblestone barriers, the faces of the people who passed me, each containing multitudes.

How long had it been since I looked, really looked, around me? In the rush of the day, how many moments were spent actively noticing the world and all that is in it? It struck me then as so beautiful, even the grime, even the grit, perhaps especially them. Every bit of broken concrete, every wrapper whipping through the wind, every crack in every foundation, the byproduct of all these people in this one magical place, trying to make a life.

I kept walking north on the west side of the street and passed some steps that led up to a church I had never noticed before. I paused, regarding them, pulled to them.

Boom, boom, boom. I felt it again, the rhythm of my heart, the beat of my body now in motion. And so slowly, I climbed the staircase. The stone was old and beautiful, worn with the weary and hopeful who had taken each step.

I walked into the church, and though I had spent my entire life devoted to God, this kind of hall of worship wasn't familiar to me. There were a few people lined up to receive confession. There were paintings of the pious and stained-glass windows that told stories of their own. Along the right wall, there was a large collection of candles, some lit, some with unburnt wicks.

I stood there, taking it in, looking at my surroundings, regarding the curves of the ceiling. I ran my eyes against the large stones on the wall, they looked cool to the touch. I ambled toward a rear pew, keeping my eyes to the ceiling.

Boom, boom, boom, my pulse quickening.

Before I could think, a prayer was on my lips.

Dear God, I made it because of you. I prayed so much, and I made it back to you. Thank you, Lord, thank you for always watching over me. For keeping the building upright long enough for me to get out. Thank you for this breath, for this moment to see this church, which I never knew existed. I am forever grateful for you and all the ways you made it happen. I am forever grateful for you and this life.

I closed my eyes, and the tears came down my cheeks. I was overwhelmed with gratitude, spilling over with thanks for having been so protected, for having been spared the fate so many found that day. My tears were clouded by the memory of a plume of smoke scorching the skyline, the stink of scalded metal, the sounds of footsteps above me that never again touched solid ground.

I stood with my eyes closed. The *boom, boom, boom* of my heart, the blood surging through my veins, had spread to my hands and up my arms. The drumbeat had dispersed into a full-body thrum. I had never felt so aware of my life, so alive in my skin.

I rested my hands lightly on the pew before me, and with my eyes closed, could feel the rivers within me. I was made of currents, the flow of my blood a powerful force within me that I had never, ever felt before. Beat by beat, inch by life-affirming inch, I could feel its rhythm through my body, up my arm, into my core, down to my toes, back up to my belly, into my head, and finally back home to my heart.

But it wasn't just the current of my blood, I realized, though that alone was a marvel. It was like pulling back the curtain of creation to see the elements that made us whole and human. It was energy. It was light. It was life itself. And it was all thanks to God.

The more I thanked and the more grateful I was, the more of my inner self I was able to feel. I wept because I never knew my body could do this; I was only here because I asked God as the tower above, beneath, and around me swayed, "*Hay Dios que hago?*" *God, what should I do?*

And God heard me and sent me a warning. As the building rumbled and fear threatened to overtake me, God answered. By muting the office, removing the sunshine and color from the room and turning it gray, God showed me there was no survival to be found in that place. And I listened, even though I was terrified. Even though I realized that in order to find life, I had to face death.

It felt like both a reminder and a lesson.

The reminder: Slow down. Find stillness. Seek peace. Ask the sacred. Look again for the answer. Look within. And listen always.

The lesson: God is not a thing to be found, an item to check off a list like a chore, a being to seek. God is not a thing or man or place or purpose. God is *us*. God is the very essence of ourselves, the energy that keeps us standing, that fuels our thinking, that brings the water that springs tears to our eyes. Faith in God is faith in our own spirit and divinity.

I never knew. Oh, God, forgive me. I never knew. I never knew my body could do this, that I could be so aware and that I could understand that you are within us all the time. That there is no separation between your spirit and me because your omniscient power is the energetic fuel of all life. My life, their lives, in this pew made of wood, in this church made of stone. In the steel that twisted in the towers. In the lives of those who were lost, but in the souls that returned home to you.

All of it. It all is a form of you, God. You are everything in this life.

Dear God, I am you, and you are me.

I sobbed, thinking of all the people who couldn't feel this, who would die, never having had the chance to know what I now knew. Those people that would never be here with us again. Sadness overwhelmed me. I couldn't catch my breath. The tears spilled out, and as I wiped them away, something changed.

Suddenly, I was back in the pew, outside of myself, no longer in the internal realm. I felt my wrist, but the energy was gone, the channel of transcendence cut. I lifted my head one last time and leaned back to that ceiling, keeping my head to the sky.

You're the most high, the all-powerful, the knower of all things, the omniscient one; I am going to leave your home now. I appreciate the silence you have given me here and this life you saved, yet once again. I know how much you truly love me and the rest of us, no matter how lost or broken. May you always know how much I love you and cherish you. How could you not know—you are always with me. I am not alone, ever. No matter what happens next, thank you for this day. Thank you, Lord. Love you. Always. Amen. Amen.

I had seen so much death, and I had been so close to my own demise, but in that church, stripped bare of the normal distractions of every day, I felt the very core of my being. On a day of so much destruction and incomprehensible loss, God was not only still present, but He was still teaching, still guiding, still loving me in the best way.

The darkness outside and in the world was a stark contrast with the light and energy within me.

I walked out of the church, pausing to look at its name: the Church of the Good Shepherd. And as I walked back into the outside world, a rush of joy swept over me. At the top of the church's staircase, I looked out onto the city block as the fresh air hit my face, and with each breath, I could sense God's presence still.

As I walked, a rush of thoughts hit me, a wave of realizations about how I had been spending my life. I could see how much I was a victim to my own vicious cycles. I could feel that the life I had been living, while it was in many ways all I had longed for, wasn't actually complete.

It didn't have to do with what I had or what I was doing. It had to do with how much I knew myself, how willing I was to recalibrate all the roots within me that led to systemic dissatisfaction. I had thought the answer to my problems—my lack of self-confidence, my inability to sit silently with my thoughts, my overwhelming self-doubt—could be fixed with a cross-country drive and a New York City address.

And while that had opened up new possibilities, it hadn't, and couldn't, solve the real issues. I was trapped in a cycle of unhappiness, the same cycle that our society is built on, that capitalism depends on. When I felt the lack of my life—not having time for what mattered, not being with the right person, not living my dreams to the fullest—I reached out for the nearest coping mechanism I could find. Smoke, work, a connection with a man—whatever filled me up and provided me with relief for even a mere moment. The more I felt, the more vices I needed to numb those feelings.

And it seemed so clear that a world designed to encourage everyone to go after these temporary solutions and to pay money for them was a world that would fold in on itself. It destroyed relationships. The fix was more important than family. Feeling good was more important than friendship. Getting what you needed to remove the ache in your heart was a higher priority than all other people on our planet.

The typical American lifestyle is built around this cycle. It doesn't matter what class, what culture, or what religion—we are all trying to fill the holes inside of us. We all do this, to some degree or another. Chasing our vices is the most vicious cycle because it's designed to keep us tamed and to keep us trapped.

The truth was simple all of a sudden: we all go without when we fail to look within.

Death is the great disruptor, the thing we are so afraid of that we spend a lifetime avoiding its name. That day, I faced it head-on, feet first, step, step, jumping away from its clutches. But even though I had escaped death today, the reflection I saw when I faced it remains.

I would remember to always take a moment to look at myself, at my life, at my past behaviors. I will balance my long-term goals with my short-term gains. I will remember that human connection, divine light, and universal energy are at the core of all that we do. I will always ask myself one question: What do I want my legacy to be?

Now that I knew the truth about God, that we were so inextricably bound together, I felt like I could see clearly. The what-ifs, the temporary lifts, the momentary distractions were not what we were put on this Earth to do or pursue.

My eyes were open. Even though I felt heavy with the immeasurable loss of that day, I was surprised to find that my spirit was light and my heart was full.

9

Home Unbound

The emerald green of Inwood Hill Park's trees was shimmering, almost dancing in the stubborn afternoon light. Inwood is home to Manhattan's oldest forest, a prehistoric relic of the time in which people lived with the land rather than built upon it. The color, Mother Nature's most natural hue, was so bright in my eyes that I had to bring up my hand to shield them. The contrast, the park's lack of gray and dust and smoke, was too great to process.

As I stepped slowly forward, my normal city walking speed clipped to a measured pace, I was struck by a sense of weightlessness. There's a game I played with my siblings when we were younger where they would lay on their backs and press their knees together, and I would lay my belly on their feet. They would grab my hands and slowly raise their legs. It made me feel like I was flying, and they would move their legs from side to side. It was the most fun game we could think of to play indoors. Fly like the condor! *Fly!*

It was the same that day as I walked through the park. The magnitude of what I had endured over the past six hours hadn't left me, and by comparison, I felt weightless. I floated above the dusty walkways, surrounded by that screaming shade of green, which seemed to move and shift of its own accord.

The trees were in full bloom on that warm September day. As I looked more closely at each leaf and limb, the light bounced off them, moved through them, and within them in such a way that I felt like it was letting me into a little universal secret. It became apparent to me that the solid structure of the leaf, veins the size of whispers and tissue-parchment-thin, were merely an illusion. Beneath them and within them, I could see that smaller particles made up their structure. I could see how a swarm of atoms banded together to create the leaf, the branch, the trunk, the tree. Looking upward at the deep cerulean sky, I saw the same—pointillism in motion, both the whole and the sum of its parts.

After what I had seen that morning, after the terror I had endured, it felt like a kindness, a gift bestowed upon me by the universe like you would give to a small child grasping to recover from disappointment. *Look*, it seemed to say, *there is still beauty to be seen. There is still so much wonder left in this world.*

As I neared the place where the road split, funneling me out of the park and back into the city, I heard a click, click, click somewhere above. I searched the trees, still undulating with the construction of particles and life, and spotted the source—a single crow, perched in a branch and peering down at me. His jet-black head twisted, his eye on mine, and I stopped to look back at him. A crow, it is believed, lives between realms, and its shining eyes can see three fates simultaneously: past, present, future. He regarded me, and I clicked back, desperate to understand how I might someday make sense of this.

I left the park behind me, passing Indian Road and up 218th Street to cross the Harlem River and get back home. Each step felt like a journey. When I reached the Broadway Bridge, I had never seen so much traffic, cars upon cars with nowhere to go. I was grateful for the freedom of the ground beneath my feet, so I decided to walk east to get some distance from the crowd and the noise. Heading east on 225th Street, I took a left on Bailey Avenue, and as I walked past Ladder 46, I couldn't shake the image of the firemen from earlier that day, my beautiful one with the knowing eyes and resolute heart.

I arrived at my building, and a sharp jolt of fear immediately cut through me.

"Oh, no! My keys!" I had grabbed my purse and sweater so quickly before sprinting out of the office that I hadn't looked to see if they were with me. I could picture them on my desk next to my uneaten breakfast, both now covered in soot and the stench of chaos.

I clambered through my purse with increasing urgency and then— gasp—a small mercy. My fingers closed over the cold metal, and I was grateful for their sharp edges against my skin. But as I slipped them into the front door lock, I was gripped by another fear. Rationally, I could see my building in front of me, but my brain could not grasp that my apartment was as I had left it that morning.

The key turned, the door unlocked, and I was inside the worn marble hallway. With each step I took, with each breath inhaled, I sniffed for smoke. I hunted for ash. All I could envision as my feet fell heavy on the steps up to my third-floor apartment was fire. All I could imagine was that the inside of my home could not have made it out unscathed and unscorched after all that had happened.

On the last flight of steps, my legs felt like they were anchored with anvils. These were not stairs I had to race down—*step, step, jump*—but that memory echoed with every heavy step I took. I was so close to home, so close to some measure of rest or solace, but I was petrified and plagued with what could be beyond the door. It wasn't rational, but nothing had made sense that day.

My front door was before me. The key fit in the lock, and the doorknob slowly turned.

But no flames flickered out to meet me. I smelled the soft scent of lavender. I saw the unfinished cup of coffee I had left on the side table before sprinting out the door that morning. I took off my shoes, walked through the French doors to my bedroom, sheets rumpled and the crescent curve of my night's rest still etched in the pillow. I sank down to my knees, grateful beyond word or measure and ran my hands over the waxed wooden floors, tracing the familiar grooves of pine. I folded my hands together, looking up to the sky, staccato breath escaping grateful lungs.

Thank you, God. Not just for coming home to such comfort but for coming home at all.

I looked across the room at the black screen of the TV in the corner, and I could see myself reflected back. *You're okay. You're safe.* But how safe was I really? I had made it out of the towers and found my way home, but what about the rest of the world?

I crawled closer to the TV and turned it on to find a channel that was covering the news, but I found that it was impossible to find one that wasn't. I landed on CNN, frantically reading the ticker tape at the bottom while listening to the commentary on screen. I could not believe what I was seeing—the Pentagon had been hit. A fourth plane had been foiled. And Tower 1, my tower, had fallen at 10:28 a.m.

Less than an hour. That handful of minutes was all that separated me from this world and the next, from sitting on my apartment floor and becoming one of the missing. The video kept showing the recap— the first plane hitting, then the second, a dark shadow careening, disappearing behind a smoking wall of glass. Tower 2 falling, imploding in on itself, and the billow of ash and wreckage that followed. Just one tower left in the sky, my tower, smoking and ripped open at the seams. I could see my floor, my window, where I had been that morning and countless mornings before.

And then it was gone. The monolith, the building that scraped the clouds, rumbled to the ground, and countless souls with it. Faces flashed before me—the Asian man who ran back into his office, the hysterical woman in the green blouse, the burned woman, the woman who had stopped to rest on the balcony, the woman who yelled at me to slow down, the firefighter with the haunted eyes. Were they still inside when the tower fell? Would I have been if I'd worn different shoes, if I hid under my desk like I had practiced as a child, if I had faltered step, step, jumping down the stairs?

I had never been so close to death or felt so far from everyone I loved. And then it hit me like a slug to the heart: *no one knows I am alive.*

Cellphones hadn't worked all morning, but I picked up my landline and dialed my father's number in Seattle. He was the hub, the one who the family would be flocking to, asking for information. If I could get word to him that I was safe, he would let everyone else know. The line was busy. I dialed again, then again and again and again, but the methodic beep was the only answer. I had been so focused on getting home that I hadn't thought about the people back home, how scared they must be, thinking about how scared I must have been. I kept calling, kept getting a busy signal until finally, I heard my dad's voice.

"Hello, I'm sorry I can't come to the phone, but ..."

"*Papi*, it's me, Annabel. I have no idea if this will get through—none of the phones are working here—but I wanted to let you know that I'm safe. I got out of the tower. I'm okay—" and the line abruptly went dead.

I tried my mother's line for hours after that, but even the beep of the busy signal had gone. The phone lines were yet another casualty of the horror of that day. I fell asleep holding the phone in my hand, desperate to get through.

I woke up in the middle of the night, jolted by the sound of a crow. My eyes sprang open as though they had just been closed moments before, but the clock said 4:35 a.m. I knew sleep wouldn't find me again that night.

I made tea, and my head swam with all that had happened—the thoughts intruded without warning—but also with everything else I had to do, like talk to my mother, get a hold of my dad, talk to my friends, and *shit*, find my brother Paul, who lived in the West Village and worked in the World Financial Center, the smallest of the four-building World Trade Center complex. From the flashes I had seen on TV yesterday, that building was still standing, but who knows where he was when we all got hit.

When the clock hit 6 a.m., I picked up my phone and dialed my mother, a caretaker for the elderly who lived upstate. After 45 minutes of trying, miraculously, the call went through.

"Hi, mom," were the only two words I could get out before I was hit with a wall of tears from the other end, a sorrow with unfathomable depths that erupted out of her. Her grief was like a storm, powerful and all-encompassing. Listening to her cry broke me open again.

When she could finally speak, she said, "*Mija, yo trate. Yo trate a verte pero... .todo estaba cerrado. Yo me fui del trabajo! Yo le dije a todos que mi hija está en las torras, y que tenía que ir allá a salvarla. Me dijeron, "Pero señora todo está cerrado! No hay buses, no hay tren, no hay ninguna persona que pueda manejar allá! No saben lo que van a hacer y la ciudad está cerrado. He sentido, que mi propio alma se me iba mi cuerpo! La angustia de no saber adónde estabas. Me sentí que estaba poniéndome loca. Mi hija y mi hijo están allí.*" Daughter, I tried. I have tried to see you... and *everything is shut down! I left! I told everyone at work, my daughter is in those towers! I have to see her and save her! They told me, 'Ma'am, we're so sorry! But everything is closed. There aren't any buses, any trains, and no one can drive to the city right now. No one knows what is happening and the city is shut down.' I have felt as if my soul was leaving me! The angst and horror of not knowing where you were. I feel like I am going crazy. Both my son and daughter down there."*

She said each word through tears, and the sound of the anguish in her voice sent chills all over my body. Her panic was so evident, her fear so palpable that I sobbed along with her, both of us weeping and wailing between words but trying to make room for her grief.

"Sentí que me estaba dando un infarto," she said. *I felt like I was having a heart attack.*

"Qué haría yo sin ti en el mundo?" she asked. *What would I do without you in the world?*

"Hay Dios te salvó mija! Gracias a Dios que te salvó y que Paul no estaba allí!" she exclaimed. *But God saved you, my daughter! Thank God he saved you and that Paul wasn't there.*

Paul, as it turns out, was in Miami. He worked for Lehman Brothers and had left on Monday night, September 10, to go to a mergers and acquisitions meeting scheduled for all day Tuesday, September 11. He had been able to get through to my mother that night to let her know he was safe and share their fear about my wellbeing. Mom had talked to him just before I called. He was renting a car to drive from Miami to New York—no planes were flying, and he needed to get home to his job, his wife Marieta, and—

"To you, Annabel," my mother said. "He said he's coming to see you as soon as he can."

Just knowing that Paul was on his way home was a balm to my grief. Paul, my big brother, who had always been my protector, had always been willing to stand up for what he believed in and for what he knew was right.

When I was in 4th grade, we lived in the Pines Apartments in Crossroads Bellevue. My sister Carol was friends with everyone, but my brother Paul was really dedicated to his studies and had a handful of close friends who didn't live in our area. They were two completely different personalities—Carol loved to dance and hang out, and Paul liked to study and play tennis. I was the youngest, often struck by the polarity of their differences, but still able to see the throughlines of our family.

One day after school, when our mom was at work, Carol, who was in 9th grade, invited a few of her girlfriends and some high school kids from the neighborhood who had never been inside our house. Paul wasn't home yet.

My friends and I were being chased around by one of the teenagers, a local kid who was friendly, and it was so much fun. He would make a yelling sound, "Haaaaaaaa!!" and we would run and scream, "Aaaaaaaaa!!" until we all landed safely in my room, hiding under the bunk bed. This went on for what seemed like hours, each time even scarier, even funnier. But then something changed. Instead of him yelling after chasing us into my room, he shut the door and pulled down his pants, exposing himself to us.

As 4th graders, none of us knew what we were looking at, and we were in shock! He was laughing, wiggling all around, and seemed to be having way too much fun with our paralysis. All of us girls were clustered under the bunk, as far back as we could go, yelling in disbelief. But no one heard us—everyone was in the living room.

But then the bedroom door opens, and in walked Paul just as the guy was pulling up his pants, laughing like crazy.

Paul asked sharply, "What are you doing there?"

"Ahh, nothing, man, just scaring the girls off by showing them my dick."

It was like a switch had been flipped.

Paul screamed, "OUT! Get out right now! What is wrong with you?!?"

Everything got quiet. Paul ushered the guy out of the house, and we followed, standing in our apartment hallway. I'd never seen my brother so mad, commanding him and everyone else to leave, due to the lines this kid had crossed, that he was never to speak with us again, that he wasn't ever welcome back into our home.

Afterward, he shut the door and came back into the house. We were milling around the hallway. Paul walked right up to me and hugged me, holding my head in his hands.

"You okay, Schnannabel?" he asked, his nickname for me that always made me smile. He ran his hand over my short brown hair, and any sense of danger or uncertainty slipped away. That was Paul, the walking moral code, the enforcer of basic respect, the protector of all he loved.

How much I needed that right now.

The phone rang, startling me, but I picked up, recognizing my father's number.

"Hello?! Dad?"

"I knew you never left," he answered.

"Oh, dad! I tried to call, but the phones didn't work."

"I know, I know. It's that way everywhere. We had problems calling, too," he sighed, exhaling his relief. "Well, you should know that your sister and Bryan woke us up early yesterday! She banged on the door, 'Dad, a plane hit the building where Annabel works.' I didn't think much of it—those buildings are strong. It must have been an accident. But Carol said, 'Dad, you have to get up and turn on the TV right now!' And when I turned on the TV, I couldn't believe it.

"Then, little by little, everyone started coming to the house. First Norma, then your Tia Elide, then Tio David. We were all there, and they were crying. But I told them, 'I am NOT going to cry. Because in my heart, I don't feel that Annabel is gone. She is still with us. And I will not shed one tear until we hear from her.'

"I kept calling different people and pacing between my office and the living room while everyone else was in the living room crying. I even had to tell them, 'If you are here in my house, stop crying, my daughter isn't dead, and I am not going to drop one tear until I hear her voice.'"

"It's so good to hear your voice, dad. I was so scared," I said, and I could hear a sharp intake of breath on the other side of the line.

"But now, now that I have you here on the phone, I can cry," he said, sobbing freely. "Because so many parents are not as lucky as I am. I still get to be your father, and you are still here to be my daughter. I love you so much."

"I love you so much, too. Thank you for everything—for your faith, for your prayers, and for waiting to hear from me. I think in many ways, knowing it gave me the strength to get out of there alive."

I told him what had happened—waking up late, looking out at the crows, that I almost didn't go into work. I told him how normal everything seemed until the unthinkable happened. I told him about no alarms, no announcements. And that is when I cried the hardest.

"They didn't do anything, dad; they didn't help us. The alarms weren't even on until the 20th floor. I was all alone. And, and the people! Those poor people ...."

I broke down. In my mind and in my heart, I knew I could tell him how I truly felt. That I couldn't believe they abandoned us. That I was unable to understand how the best military in the world couldn't stop the plane. That I felt alone still, even though I was safe in my apartment.

That I shuddered with fear and ducked my head every time a military plane went overhead. That I couldn't bring myself to set foot outside.

"I know, Annabel," my dad said, calming me down. "You need rest, *mija*. Come stay here for a while. We want to take care of you."

"I want to, dad, but I can't leave everything."

"I understand," he replied. "Just know we are here."

We said goodbye, but that was the last phone call I took that day. People were desperate to reach each other, and though the phone lines were spotty, if you were persistent, you could eventually get through. My voicemail was full and hearing the voices of my friends and other members of my family warmed my heart, but they all had the same questions. *What happened? How did you get out? What did you see? How are you doing? Just calling to tell you we love you and have been praying for you.*

I couldn't answer—I'd quickly become overrun with flashes of memories that brought me right back into the fear and fire. I let people know I was okay but didn't share more. It was as much for me as it was for them—the horror wasn't easy to hold.

The rest of the day was a blur, but I eventually slept, opening my tired eyes, unsure of where I was or the time. I stretched tentatively, reaching out my limbs one by one. I felt the familiar stir of my soft Egyptian cotton sheets, a deep burgundy the color of ripe pomegranate seeds, which were usually a comfort, but were now damp with the twists and turns of nightmares.

The sun cracked through the drawn curtains. A single ray cast down, and I reached my hand up to touch it. I could feel its warmth, the way it seared through the darkness and the chill of the morning. I let my hand dance with the beam, my fingers, rosy with short white nails, stretching and uncurling as the light played with each knuckle and skittered across my skin. I stared captivated at the deep red lines of each finger, the etches in my palm, the flow of my blood. Were these really my hands? Had they grasped the ashy railings in the stairwell? When was the last time they had touched someone else's skin? Would my blood and body ever feel as alive as it had in the church the day before?

My hands sliced through the single stream of sun, and I breathed in the air all around me. It was soft and clear. It smelled like home. I was overwhelmed, both with gravity and with gratitude. My first thought was: I am alive. And my second: so many are not.

I fell on my hands and knees, bowing down on my elbows and forearms, and thanked God for saving me. So humbled, so crushed, as tears fell, knowing that even in that moment, in that despair, that I was *blessed* to be in despair. That I was blessed to be able to pray, to cry for those who weren't so lucky.

But my gratitude was eclipsed by questions: Are we at war? What is happening in the world? Is the stock market back? What is happening with work now that the whole office is gone?

I tried to take care of the essentials, the routines: take a shower, get dressed, organize, clean, anything to keep my mind off of the thoughts that were always just below the surface. But they always bubbled right back up again.

What if they attack us? What if our currency changes out of spite for Saudi Arabia and OPEC? What if they bomb us and really take us out? If they can't protect the World Trade Center, how could they possibly protect the Bronx?

Later that day, I heard more fighter jets sear the sky above us, a true novelty in the city, especially given the lack of commercial jets and helicopters. Growing up in Seattle, there was a summer festival called SeaFair on Lake Washington, a festival of sorts with stands of food, games, and people all together on the water having fun. The highlight of the day was always the Blue Angels, their beautifully choreographed flights dancing above us. I had always loved the sound they made—the roar and the woosh.

But now, hearing that sound, I ducked my head, sprinted for my backpack, and tried to resist the urge to sprint out the door. The skies above were full with the vibration of air, of speed, of motion.

That sound! *Vrooooooooom!* I heard the planes, and the hairs on my skin stood at attention. Another attack felt imminent. My apartment was on a street called Albany Cres, which was shaped like a crescent moon and sitting right on top of Highway 87, "The Major Deegan." My thoughts wandered to strategy—if anyone wanted to shut off traffic to and from the city, this spot would be ideal.

I jumped to my feet, grabbed my bag, ran to my front door, and threw open the stairwell window. I stood in my apartment doorway and listened for the roar of bombs, for the sound of screaming.

But those sounds never came, and as the sound of the jet faded, I was able to breathe again. I turned on the radio and then the TV for any mention of war, but the news was just news, and slowly my heart stilled, and my head filled up with the noise of the television.

I was on the razor's edge of fight or flight, and it drained me, being so on the verge of disaster. Any energy I'd woken up with was gone. I had lost all momentum, and the only thing I seemed capable of was lying down. I put my head on the pillow. The view out my window was sunny and clear.

I don't remember falling asleep, but soon I was surrounded with the whispers of the unseen, with the faces of the people who perished, the feeling of souls all around me. *I'm so sorry*, I said in dreams. *I'm so sorry I am not doing more with my day, with my life. I'm just so tired.*

When I woke, I didn't want food. I didn't want friends. I just wanted to be able to focus on something, on anything, to have the sharpness of my thoughts return, to not feel so dulled by circumstances and stress that my mind was paralyzed.

I felt compressed like I was in between the people in the sky, the souls who I felt in the high rise now in the clouds and the world before me. I felt so heavy, so incapable, so broken down by the frantic activity of the world, but that was nothing compared to the storm that raged inside me, lighting thoughts and thunderous emotions until I could do nothing but scream to give them somewhere to go.

The next day, there was a knock on the door. I opened it to my brother Paul, and all I could do was hug him and fall into his arms. It felt so good to be held, so good to be near someone I had known for my whole life, so good to be reminded of the world outside. After a few minutes, we walked down the hallway and into my living room.

"Did you really drive all the way from Miami?"

He nodded as we settled on the couch. "I got the last rental car in Miami. I had to get back here to make sure you were all right."

Paul had first seen the towers during a breakfast business meeting meant to discuss a merger and acquisitions deal. He saw the plane hit the second building, the flames engulf the top stories, but when the first tower fell, he told his colleagues. "My sister works there. I need to get back."

He left first thing the next morning and drove as fast as safely possible before getting into the city in the wee hours of Friday morning.

"I drove through the Lincoln Tunnel, and when I came out the other side, the towers were gone—it looked like someone punched the city's teeth clear out of the sky," he said. "But as much as that scared me, nothing scared me more than thinking about you inside those towers. What happened?"

Maybe it was because he was there in person, maybe it was because of our family bond, but I told Paul everything, each moment as much as

I could bare, in each piece. We spoke for hours, and sharing those details with him, unloading the story from my brain and into the hands, head, and heart of someone so dear to me, felt like therapy.

Just as the sun started to fade a bit, I told him about being in the church and feeling my blood and God within me. I let the tears flow freely. I let my breath catch in my throat. I let the sobs escape, and my body shiver. He stood, pulling me close to him and holding my head to his shoulder, his hand on my hair.

"I understand," he said, his own tears spilling down. "I feared that I wouldn't see you again."

With each sentence, I could feel his chest quake, but his hand steadily touched my hair, the most merciful comfort.

"Everyone prayed for you," he continued. "I can't believe how blessed we are to have our prayers answered. My biggest prayer ever fulfilled was having you still here as my sister.".

I was safe. My brother was always there for me, holding me, crying with me, sharing my burden.

"Shhh," he said. "You are safe, my Schnannabel."

And I laughed for the first time in a long while.

I slept soundly that night for the first time since I woke up on that Tuesday morning. Two weeks passed in my apartment, each day the same cycle of gratitude, frenetic activity, distraction, desperation, fear, and exhaustion. Time was stretched and stunted all at once, days slipping into weeks, minutes melting into hours.

One morning, light streamed in between the cracks of my curtained bedroom windows, and I knew the day was going to be different. Today I was going to have a visitor, the first one since my brother Paul.

My nephew Bryan was coming to the city—my sister and my mom were on their way to France for a long-planned trip. Undeterred by any reverberations from the 11th, somehow able to push through whatever faraway fear they had, they hopped on a plane to cross the Atlantic and arrived safely on the other side. Bryan disembarked in NYC and was promptly picked up by my brother. It had been arranged long before that Bryan would stay with me, so eager was I to have some quality time with this young boy suddenly on the cusp of becoming a man.

I rose out of bed, spurred on by an actual item on my to-do list, and my head swam with the thought of human interaction. When I opened the door for him later that night, I couldn't believe how tall he'd gotten.

"Tia!" he yelled.

We hugged, and I was reminded of his gentle spirit. I welcomed him in, took his bags, and showed him to the pullout bed I'd set up for him in the living room.

"What can I get you?" I asked, relieved to be thinking about someone else's needs.

"Oh, it's so late, Tia. It's been a long day. Is it okay if I just hit the sack?"

"Of course," I responded. "We'll have a fun day tomorrow."

He didn't know, of course, what a shut-in I had become, how hard things had been. Just his presence was like a buoy, bringing me up from the depths I had been under.

He got ready for bed, and I tucked him in, just like I had done countless times when he was a child. I gave him a kiss on the forehead.

"Sleep well," I said. "Have good dreams."

As I crawled into my own bed just a room away, I wondered what tomorrow would bring. It had been so long since I'd seen anyone, done anything, been able to cross over the threshold of my apartment and into the world that I wondered if I was capable of it. Would I emerge from this traumatic chrysalis a transformed creature? Or would I run back inside to the ramshackle refuge I'd found?

10

Unsettled Hearts

A scream echoed through the apartment.

"Put her out! Put her OUT!" A sob followed, wrenched from the depths of sleep, and I sat up, drenched in sweat.

I struggled to catch my breath and get my bearings. The dream had felt so real, dredged up directly from memory, the burning woman in the stairwell etched into the folds of my subconscious. In the dream, she stared at me, terrified and engulfed in flame, and no matter how fast I jumped or how hard I pushed people aside, I couldn't reach her. But her eyes never left me, and I couldn't look away.

"Tia?" I heard in a soft angelic voice. I looked up, and Bryan was in my doorway, his big eyes lovingly staring at me.

"I'm so sorry, Bryan," I said, tears brimming while feeling so grateful for the darkness so he couldn't see them. "I'm so sorry I woke you."

"Don't worry about me, Tia. Are you okay?"

"I'm okay," I answered, a reassurance for him but also for myself. I felt terrible he was here to witness this, to see how scared and scarred I had become. He was too young for all of this. "Having you here, I feel better already. Look at the smile you already put on my face."

I went to him and hugged him, and it truly felt like medicine.

"Time for sleep," I said.

"Sweet dreams," he replied.

But only a few hours later, my voice cut through the darkness again.

"I will go wherever the fuck I want to go, and you can't stop me!"

I woke up to bright lights and Bryan standing over me with tears in his eyes, his palm on my forehead.

"Tia, Tia, it's okay. You're dreaming. It's just a dream."

I was fully awake but couldn't shake the images that played through my mind. My breath came in jagged measures, too quick and too shallow. I put my head on the pillow and cried.

"I'm so sorry, Bryan, I just need to lie down," I got out between sobs. "Please go back to bed. I'm so sorry you have to see this. I had no idea this was going to happen."

He gave me a quick, sweet kiss on the cheek and went back to the living room. Sleep found me again, but the respite was short. Two hours later, I was up again, my sheets twisted in a sweat-soaked knot, my limbs tired from thrashing around. The light in the living room was on, but I was alone. I turned on the radio to find some comfort in the dulcet tones of the deejay's midnight shift, so tired but too scared to sleep again. I must have drifted off because I woke up to the familiar smell of tea.

Bryan and I sipped slowly around my small kitchen table.

"It's good," I said with gratitude in each syllable.

"Are you good, Tia?" he asked tentatively.

"I'll be okay," I replied, not because I was, but because I had faith I would be. I had to. It was all I had left.

"Let's go out," I said to Bryan.

"Okay," he responded simply as if it weren't the bravest thing I had said for the past month. As though it was normal, which made me feel a bit more like I was. "Where to?"

"Out!" I yelled from the hallway as I grabbed my jacket.

We walked outside, just the two of us in a sea of trees and people. The fresh air felt like a relief. My senses started to open up again, the crispness of an October breeze, the bounce and give of the dirt and earth beneath our feet, the sounds of scurrying creatures who had made their home in the biggest city in the world. We spent hours walking and talking, bouncing around the Bronx, stopping to see what caught our attention, hitting up some of my favorite haunts, just enjoying being together. We walked east on Kingsbridge Road so I could take Bryan school shopping for clothes.

On our way back home, we found a tiny blue building on the edge of the sidewalk in the middle of the hood on Fordham Avenue, a grid of opaque windows on each side. A large sign read "US Armed Forces Recruiting Center," and through the propped door, I could see two young men standing inside—one an African American-looking brother and the other a light-skinned brother with long black braids. I couldn't tell if they were Afro-Latinos or not, but either way, they were young men with their whole lives in front of them, and the thought of them being mentally, emotionally, and physically tortured by memories of war just made my body so hot, and my heart grew heavy.

Oh, no, was all I could think as I took a deep breath. I imagined the terror they would experience if they signed up and went to war. It seemed imminent, palpable like it was on the tip of the world's tongue.

"Come on, Bryan," I said without thinking, and I marched us both inside. It was bigger than it looked from the street, so I made him sit in the corner as far away from everyone else as possible.

The recruiter, a stocky, square-shaped man with a blond crewcut flecked with gray, was speaking with the two men, barely boys I could see now that I was close enough to judge the softness of their cheeks. They were mid-conversation, and I recognized the determination the two boys had in their eyes. You don't walk into a recruitment center without a fire inside you that needs to be fanned.

I stepped up to them.

"We do love our men and women who proudly serve," I said. I looked directly at the recruiter, adding, "Thank you for all you do for our country. I came in here today because I know how hard it is right now, but know this: we have been attacked, and we will be at war soon."

"You don't know that," the recruiter answered. "We are not at war right now."

But inside me, inside the smokey staircase of One World Trade Center, the war had already been waged. What I experienced for a few hours, these young men were signing up to experience for months, perhaps years. Would they die? Who could say? But who they were as people would wilt and morph and shift into something unrecognizable. Whatever promise was being sold to them was not worth the price their souls would have to pay.

That's the biggest fallacy of war that we think it's normal, that it's the justifiable action that follows an unjust act. But if you play it out further, every group of people in power could wield it to kill another group, and then who is left?

I looked at Bryan and remembered when he was little, the two of us sitting on a rug with his toys, me reminding him how to share his blocks, how to take turns. It's interesting that we still teach our children to share, but we have such a hard time with it as adults. Most of the time, in war, we are fighting for something we want—a commodity, a border, a right. We fight just to take. We hit first and ask questions later.

We destroy in the name of gain or pain. And in doing so, we destroy ourselves.

"You don't have to do this," I said softly to the two young men.

The recruiter piped up. "They'll get opportunities with us that they can't get here. If he serves, he can get funding to go to college and build a better life for himself and his family."

"Sure, he can," I responded. "But at what price? The college fund doesn't kick in until after you serve in active duty, and though we may not be at war now, we all know it's only a matter of time. How dare you ask them to sacrifice their sanity, their lives. Have you experienced that amount of death? Have you been kept awake by the faces of the ones whose lives were lost? And when you do sleep, do you wake up screaming?"

"Ma'am, I think I'm going to have to ask you to leave."

"Sir, this is a public building, paid for by our tax dollars, and I will not leave until I am finished," I said. I turned to the two young men. "Listen to me. I used to work in the World Trade Center. I was on the 46th floor of Tower 1, and I was one of the lucky ones. I made it out on September 11th, but so many others were not so lucky. It's the most horrific experience to be attacked, to see that violence firsthand." My voice was steady, my resolve strong. Everyone was quiet and still.

"You don't have to do this. You have so many other options with this one precious life. Please," I said. Begging, pleading, looking at the two young men with all the honesty I could manage while still managing to hold myself together. I painted such a vivid picture of what would await them the terror, the pain, the constant assault on life as they knew it.

The darker, more African-looking brother didn't break eye contact. I could see that he felt me, that he felt my agony and understood my relentlessness. He stood up, smacked his lips, and with a look on his face like, "*Shit, this sister just saved me from hell!*" he walked out without a word.

"Ma'am," said the recruiter. Bryan walked closer to me, "Tia, we gotta go."

I turned to the other one, this tall young man with fresh braids and fresh Timbs, dressed in snap sweatpants and a Phat Farm shirt, but he wouldn't look at me.

"Okay, sir," I replied but kept my eyes on the recruit. "The war ahead of us could be an endless war. You have a family, don't you? You can go to college now, can't you? You don't need the Army to live the life you want. Just please, give yourself time. Don't sign up yet."

The recruiter stood up and moved toward me. Bryan stood up a split-second later, moving toward me.

"Tia," said Bryan, his face red. "Let's go!"

Together, we strode out onto the street. We walked west, battling the blowing wind, feeling the weak rays of the sun in the advent of fall. The crisp air held back my tears, and I grabbed Bryan's hand, looking both ways.

"It's safe. Let's cross."

When we arrived on the other side of the street, Bryan let go of my hand and began jumping up and down, laughing.

"I can't believe you, Tia! You just totally convinced that guy! And that wasn't enough—you went two for two!"

I stopped and looked at him directly in the eyes. "You know I love this country. You know I am proud of all the people who serve. But right now, Bryan, there is too much pain and no place to put it. People will channel that into conflict, and we will go to war. I don't wish that on anyone. Maybe all they needed was someone to show them another way. I just worry so much... I don't want anyone to have to see what I've seen."

"I know what will help," he said. "Let's get some food."

We went to Broadway Pizza in Kingsbridge and picked up a few slices. As we were walking home, we passed a black minivan that had white spray paint emblazoned on the back window: *We don't want you Muslims here. Go home, murderers!*

We kept walking. Bryan was talking in his usual animated way, taking bites as he spoke, relishing some real New York pizza. But I was too lost in thought to eat. My mind was back at the minivan, marveling at how quickly hate had taken hold. The actions of a few had already led to the condemnation of a whole religion. We arrived at my building, and even though I had more right to be angry than many people did—I had seen firsthand the devastation that was born of hatred—I couldn't find it anywhere even remotely in my soul to harbor that kind of hatred. My skin burned as though I was back in the tower near the blaze.

"Bryan, stay here."

"What's going on, Tia?"

"I just need to get something quickly. Take my keys, go inside, and finish your food. I'll be right back."

I got him inside and spun on my heels, my slice still in my hands. I sprinted down the stairs—*step, step, jump*—and back to the street. In under a minute, I was back at the van, and somehow the normally crowded avenue was almost completely empty. I stared at the words: *We don't want you Muslims here. Go home, murderers!*

I could think only of the injustice, of how many wrongs Christians had unleashed on the world, how much suffering. And yet, Christians weren't hated because of their slaughter, their swift vengeance and fierce wars. How easy it was to hate the "other," the ones who don't look like us or worship like us; and judge them all for what a few do.

I longed for a hammer to smash that window, for spray paint to cover it up. But in the absence of those, I used what I could—I took the slice of pizza in my hands and smeared all those hateful words until they were illegible. My dinner was a small sacrifice to pay for some semblance of peace.

I went back home, and Bryan opened the door for me.

"What happened, Tia?"

"I shared my pizza with some people who really needed it," I told him.

Bryan spent a week at my place, and little by little, we expanded our footprint outside my door. I grew more comfortable with being in the world, and at the end of the week, I took him down to my brother Paul and his wife Marieta's place at the Biltmore Plaza on 29th Street and 3rd. They lived in a one-bedroom apartment with a sliver view of the East River. Bryan was set to leave the next day, and I had a doctor's appointment early the next morning, so we all spent the night together, Paul and Marieta in their bedroom, me on the couch, and Bryan on a makeshift bed near the windows.

It was the first time I had spent the night in a bed that wasn't my own since before September 11th, and sleep didn't find me easily. I was bone-tired, drained from attempting to interact normally with people, even these people I so deeply love. Their lives hadn't been shattered, and though their care for me could barely be contained, it felt impossible to share what was echoing in my own mind and heart—the fear, the ceaseless worry, the fight-or-flight mechanism on constant overdrive.

I woke up around 6:15 a.m. after a handful of hours of sleep and silently padded out of the apartment to make my way to the top floor for a solo swim. The ceiling had windows that looked out to the sky, and an indoor pool stretched the length of the building. I was alone, and I took a deep breath before flexing my toes and diving deep into the water. The night before had been the first time sleeping away from my apartment, and this was the first time I was fully submerged since before the attacks.

Life after the 11th was a process of rediscovery—what feels different, what feels the same. How my outlook has been altered, how my core has kept its shape. And worse, where it had been fractured.

Water is such an interesting thing. Floating there, my face up to the skylights with the sun's refracted rays bouncing off the surface of the pool and my skin, I felt a deep comfort. My body was weightless, but it was my soul that so briefly felt lighter as if the pressure of the water all around me held me together well enough that it finally was given permission to rest.

How fast could I swim, I wondered. I used to be a good swimmer, back in the apartment complex pools and the wild Pacific Ocean. Here, on the other side of America, I reached backward, my hands shaped like paddles, and pushed the water down. It had been years, but it came back so easily, this favorite backstroke. I relaxed, stretching out my muscles and limbs, my head steady at the sky. I could feel when I was close to the wall, and my body twisted in response. Head down, right hand up, left hand up, head turned to breathe. Two more strokes, then head pivot to the right. Soon I was speeding, cutting through the water with deliberate strokes and all my might, breathless but determined.

When my body tired, I got out of the pool to get ready. This doctor's appointment had been hanging on my calendar for months, a date seemingly far away for ages.

My doctor, a mature, strong woman whose face was an exercise in symmetry, worked at NYU Hospital on the east side of lower Manhattan on William Street, right in the middle of downtown. A cab would never make it—the whole of downtown was still blocked off for cleanup—so I got onto the subway. I got out at City Hall, and when I surfaced to the street level, the smell hit me first, unmistakable. Sharp, acrid, chemical, and charred, the smoke seeming to have settled into the city itself. There was no billowing cloud, no wafts of green or gray streaking the wind, but the bricks were infused with it. The stones were saturated. The air itself had swallowed so much of it that it seemed to seep out of the sky.

As I walked down Park Rowe, I was stepping closer and closer to the Twin Towers. In my mind, I couldn't picture the cityscape without them, but I looked over from Spruce Street, and there it was— Manhattan's still-open wound. A single billowing thread of smoke streamed out of the rubble, a steady eruption of despair. I looked up in a kind of dreadful wonder, searching for where the towers had been. My memories were so strong—I could still see myself sitting at my desk in my office, the pieces of which were floating somewhere in the soot that hung overhead and crept into my senses uninvited. The reality in front of me was too stark a contrast, the empty sky, the stench of smoke, a city fundamentally changed. I turned the corner, walking down the next street with my eyes still on the skyline. I had been living inside for the past month, thinking of the towers constantly, replaying my escape, but also thinking of the time spent inside them, my daily routine. The disbelief at seeing a clear sky where there should be the two tallest buildings in the city was overwhelming and disorienting. I tripped on the pavement underfoot.

I found my doctor's building by blindly following the street names and numbers until I stumbled inside. I waited to be seen, and when my name was called, the routine of it all—the rote questions, the rhythm of health and wellness—lulled me into normalcy. When my body passed its tests, Dr. Cohen looked at me and said she wasn't going to be practicing there any longer.

"Are you going to another hospital in the city?" I asked.

She shook her head. "No, I'm going back home to Israel, where I was born, to be with my people."

"That's a big move."

"It is," she said. "But with everything that has happened, I know exactly where I need to make sure we are strong enough to handle it if something happens again."

"I wish you all the best," I replied and meant it. She was the only other person I had met in the past weeks whose life had also been inexorably changed by the attacks we had endured. I thought about her frequently in the days that followed, about her decision to leave. Terror had put her on a different path. Where might it take me?

Back in my apartment, struggling to make sense of the days again, I heard the news that the Federal Emergency Management Association and the American Red Cross had set up a tent in Manhattan to offer support to those who needed it. Sick of being stagnant, I went down one afternoon to find out more and see what my options were. Walking along Riverside, I saw a huge white encampment, bigger than a stadium, across the West Side Highway, which seemed as wide as a river.

I was nervous. It was like approaching a scene from a science fiction movie. I followed the signs and arrived at the processing table. I went up to its edge and said, "Hi, I'm Annabel. I heard you might be able to help survivors?" They had all this paperwork, piles of it, sorted by the letter of your last name. I filled it out dutifully and was let inside. It was almost like a flea market, with different sections and stalls—seating areas, water and food stations, the medical bay, massage tables, therapists, religious leaders, housing, unemployment—all separated by pipe draping.

Each service had its own application. I had food, a roof over my head, my faith—but what I needed desperately was help with my own mind, with my emotions, with the ways I couldn't shake it from my body. I brought my application to the man in charge of resourcing therapists, and after glancing over the first few pages, his eyes snapped up at me.

"You were inside the tower when the planes hit?"

"Yes." I turned red hot in my face.

"Hold on. Wait right here," he said as he jumped up and rushed off to a small group of people. At the same time, all three of them looked over at me, the way you might regard a ghost. They finished their conversation, and he came back over to me.

"Follow me, please."

"Sure," I said and followed him beyond the curtain wall and through a fabricated maze. He brought me over to a woman named Catherine, who was middle-aged, white, and had straight dirty-blonde hair. She was so full of kindness that it seemed to spill out of her, and with each question she asked, I was more thankful I had come.

Catherine promised assistance but stated they couldn't truly help unless I had a letter from my own therapist certifying that I had a diagnosis of post-traumatic stress disorder. That diagnosis, a common condition among returning combat veterans, would then allow me to access the full spectrum of Salvation Army support. But without that, I was back where I started.

"I'm sorry we can't handle this for you," said Catherine. "We used to have therapists on staff but not anymore. There's only so much people can handle."

Tell me about it, I thought but did not say.

They gave me everything, a thick white folder complete with all the details and next steps. I called my therapist, who was across the street from a McCormick & Schmick's steakhouse on the east side in Midtown, and made an appointment. I had only seen her a few times, months ago, but now I needed her again.

"Okay, Annabel, I'll see you," she said. "But please know that it will be $100 a visit if you don't have insurance."

I swallowed hard. "I understand," I said, even though I was out of work, had no insurance, and had very little money. "I need to see you."

Her office was marked with a shiny silver awning on the street entrance. I walked into the familiar entryway that felt like a museum—floor-to-ceiling marble dotted with flecks of color. It was older, but it was clean. Though I had been here before, there was little comfort in stepping back into the building.

I pressed the button to the top floor, but when the doors opened, I couldn't bring myself to step out. Her office was set up like a residence. The living room had dark marble and rock floors, deep gray furniture and accents, and the occasional splash of blood red for color contrast. The heavily curtained windows were cracked open to look out onto the sky. I hadn't been on a floor this high since the 11th.

"Come on in, take a seat," said a raspy, grounded voice with a thick New York accent. "I'll be with you in a moment." She was petite, short, Jewish, and in her early 60s, a lifelong New Yorker. The degrees printed and framed on the walls were an ever-present reminder of her educational prowess. As usual, all of it intimidated me.

As I waited, I thought about the therapy appointments I'd had in the past. I had done what I thought everyone was supposed to do—talked about my childhood, the complex relationships I had with members of my family, the scars I had accumulated throughout the years. But now, those topics felt insufficient. I knew I just needed a letter, but how could I begin to discuss the multitude and magnitude of emotions that screamed inside me?

And the second that thought entered my mind, the feelings came rushing in—anxiety, terror, nervousness, panic, loneliness, guilt, sadness. I felt so exposed here, so high above the floor, so far from my apartment, the one solace I had found. How do you start to talk about something that has taken over who you are?

She sat down, and I started speaking about the news. Rushing, talking about the city, the military, can you believe all the soldiers in the city? Can you believe the skyline will never be the same? That this happened at all? That this had never happened before? Can you believe we will soon be at war? The words tumbled out one after the other, thoughts of government and power, of battle and the bravery we expect, of the horror that the struggle for power brings to the people.

"I'm sorry," she said, and for a brief moment, I felt like maybe she understood.

"I'm sorry, too."

"No, Annabel. I'm sorry because we're out of time."

I couldn't believe 45 minutes had passed—for all the fears inside my heart, I had spoken mostly with my mind.

"And I'm sorry, too, that I won't be writing you a letter today."

"But I need that letter to get help!"

"You don't have PTSD," she said confidently. "You may be scared of war, but you weren't in one. It actually sounds like you've got everything figured out just fine."

She smiled, but it was hollow.

"Now, as we discussed, that will be $100."

I fumbled to get my checkbook out, my hands trembling with rage and disbelief. What exactly was I paying her for? What was I supposed to do now?

I slowly, deliberately ripped the check out along the perforated lines and placed it on the table in front of her. I couldn't even look at her; I just placed it on the table and left. I never wanted to see her again.

Why wouldn't she help me? Did she get upset with me worrying about war and talking about it? I couldn't speak about the day itself; it was just too much. What was I going to do? I was out of money, I had no letter, and I needed to have another FEMA meeting. How was I going to get help? The American Red Cross wouldn't help me; no one was helping me, even though everyone was donating millions to the American Red Cross.

A week or so passed. I called so many places but eventually focused my efforts on Montefiore in the Bronx for one key reason: it was free. I had been out of work for weeks. But after dozens of calls, I received one back. The lady I talked to was very nice, if overwhelmed, and I shared both that I needed to speak with someone and that I would need a letter.

"Is that something you can do for me?" I asked, my voice shaking slightly.

"Yes, of course," she replied through the line. "That is what we do."

My sigh of relief filled up the room.

A few days later, I took the bus across town. I hadn't ever been on the east side of the Bronx until then. When I got there, I didn't realize it was the whole hospital. The room was stark, sterile, and smelled like rubbing alcohol.

The woman I met had a happy and compassionate spirit. She was older than me, and her hair was pulled back, but her spirit shone through; she was clearly young at heart.

"I'm Annabel," I said, reaching for her hand.

"I remember your voice from the phone!" she exclaimed, taking my hand in both of hers as we shook. "Oh, what you have been through."

"You remember me?"

"Of course, I do! How could I forget? Now tell me whatever it is that is weighing on you. I would imagine it's quite a lot."

That morning, the calendar had turned to November, and I needed this letter from her to move forward, to get help, to try to process everything and live my life in a new way. But I was so scared to share again, and my stomach flipped at the thought of another wasted session.

She started small with a seemingly simple question: "How are you?"

So I just shared with her where I worked, what was happening that morning, how I had escaped. Sticking to the facts, I ran through everything I had been doing and coping with since.

"The days are all just melting together into one long day. I read about the markets, the news. I take long walks up at Van Cortlandt Park and work out because I can't sleep for nights at a time. My mind keeps thinking we'll be attacked again, so I just try to anticipate it by reading about what Congress is doing, what the oil markets are doing, trying to keep up with our foreign policy discussions. I don't want to be blind-sided again…and my emotions overwhelm me. I just feel too much, then I feel exhausted, then numb, like I'm just watching the world before me. I can't concentrate; even simple tasks at home become a mission and take me all day. I really don't know how to answer that question… how am I? I am different, and I don't know what to do."

I expected the same blank stare as from the previous therapist, but instead, she offered the two warmest words I had heard in a long while: "I understand." She added, "I can't imagine what you've been through, but you have experienced extreme acute trauma. What you are grappling with is real and deep, but I'd like to help you. When can we set up another session?"

"Next week or the following week?" I replied, and then, in the same tone a teenager might ask her crush out on a first date, I asked, "But do you think you might be able to write me a letter? I need help from FEMA, and in order to get that, I need a letter from you.

"Of course! You're alive! And what a brilliant, lucky thing!" she exclaimed. "But that doesn't mean life is easy now. Everything you shared is a part of PTSD. I'll work on the letter and mail it to you when it's done."

Walking out of her office, I had to stop to lean against the stark white wall. It was the first time I had said all of that out loud at once, that I had let those demons and worries fly into the world. But that wasn't what stopped me. What stopped me was the slow creep of a new emotion. Somewhere buried deep down in the slurry of worry and dread, hope had taken root and started to bloom.

I received the letter from the counselor a week later and headed back quickly to the FEMA camp to get the help I was promised. I walked in and found the registration table again.

"I'm here for assistance," I said, explaining who I was, what happened the last time I was there, what I was hoping for now.

"I'm so sorry," said the kind stranger after reviewing my paperwork. "The deadline has passed."

"What does that mean?" I asked, disbelieving.

"We can't help you. I'm so sorry."

I was despondent, after all the hoops I had leaped through, all the ways I felt unable to function, yet had somehow done exactly what I was supposed to. And then this? And then…nothing?

I turned to leave, deflated.

"Wait!" the stranger exclaimed, and he held out his hand to slip me a small piece of paper, the way you would give someone a conspiratorial folded note in grade school. I opened it back home, and inside it was a short verse from Leviticus 19:16: *You shall not stand idle while your neighbor bleeds.*

I made a cup of hot tea, the rising steam and liquid warmth a balm, and I turned those words over in my mind. It was meant, I think, as a plea to incite action against the men who had fundamentally altered our lives, my life. Our American neighbors were bleeding, our fellow New Yorkers, and, yes, they were helping. But they weren't helping me, a survivor, a casualty of this instant war, and where had they been in the past? How many times had our nation failed its own citizens, failed to protect each other, failed to stop our collective bleeding?

I thought, as I often did, about the men who bombed the towers, who worshiped in a different faith altogether and decided they likely lived by those same words: *You shall not stand idle while your neighbor bleeds.* But it felt so misguided, the barriers between us so flimsy and false. What good are those imaginary lines that separate us? If everyone looked out for each other, arms open instead of up in arms, how would that change the world and the worlds we each contain within ourselves?

I have always believed that if we do not look within, we go without. What did I need to heal? How could I mend the bleeding in my own broken soul? It was clear to me that no one in the city was going to help me. How could I help myself?

The answer came in four letters, a small word for such a big place. It pulled on each broken heart string like the tug of an umbilical cord.

I called my father, who picked up on the first ring.

"Hi, *papi*," I said. "Dad, I think it's time to come home."

11

Trees and Mountains

I felt pulled to the West Coast—come home, come home. Come back to where you were born.

I left on November 16, 2001, just over two months from when the towers fell. I had been so scared to fly, but the need to be back was strong enough that I summoned the courage to step onto my flight, find my window seat, and settle in.

We took off without incident and headed west. Looking out my tiny window, I saw a shimmering river shaped like a snake, weaving through the plains and mountains below. How beautiful water is—it takes so many shapes, it's so flexible yet strong. The sunlight hit it in such a way that it looked as though the water had turned to gold, the commodity we chased so freely and foolishly, when in actuality, water is the thing that gives us food, runs through our veins, and gives us life.

Life. That was what I was seeking—a real life, not just the husk that I had barely held together the past few months. I was searching for healing, for love from family and friends, the hug of Mother Nature in the familiar terrain of the Pacific Northwest. But mostly, I think, I was searching for myself.

Looking out the plane window, I thought of a past boyfriend, Cam. We met at Art Bar, and we'd always see each other dance, but we never quite connected until the day he showed up with a book: *The Bible Code*, by Michale Drosnin.

He pressed it into my hands and said, "Read this. Then come back and talk to me."

I knew he was kickin' it to me, but he looked at me so sincerely and spoke with such confidence that I couldn't dismiss him, so we talked. And when most guys talk the talk, you realize they're all hype, but not so with Cam. We became friends, and one rainy night, we kissed and never looked back.

We would read together, cuddled close under blankets, books in each of our hands. We read many things, but we focused much of our time on our spirit. Cam was the first man I ever fell in love with because of his grounded mind. He was so different than everyone I had dated before—smart, sensitive, insightful. We would dance together, read together, and soon enough, we even meditated together.

He helped me try on different faiths to see what truly fit. At one point, I was very interested in learning about Islam, and for a month, I wore a hijab wherever I went. I read the Quran several times, each time inspired, each word a whole different lens with which I could see God, humanity, and truth. Cam wasn't Muslim, but he always respected my faith journey, and he never wondered why all of a sudden, I was practicing something new. He respected my choices and helped me to pursue the path I was on.

But soon, I found there were parts of the Islamic religion that didn't resonate deeply with me. I found more questions than answers, most around the concept of man-made law vs. foundations of faith, and this exploration sparked something in me. I started lining up all the man-made rules in religion and separating them from God's law, which is universal. Anytime one law or rule gives power to one sex or one culture, it felt man-made, and I couldn't embrace words I didn't understand. If the law serves all people, then that is God's law, universal. I could not put all my faith in one religion because too many beliefs fell on the wrong side of that tally.

Together, Cam and I read books that opened my mind to different ways of thinking about God and opened up new pathways to explore the fundamental questions I had always had about my own spiritual upbringing. But when we read *Conversations with God* by Neale Donald Walsch, my soul screamed, "Yes!" As I read the words about one man's year of direct dialog with God, I realized that no single religion could fulfill my heart. I needed my spiritual roots, but I searched to find other ways to spread my wings and deepen my relationship with our Creator.

I knew my spiritual self couldn't grow until I understood myself beyond simply a human being, a realization that came to me when I meditated for the first time. At night, we'd put on guided meditation tapes and sit together in the dark, focusing on our breathing, practicing letting our thoughts go. Cam announced to me one day that he was off to a far corner of Washington State to do a 10-day meditation, during which not a word would be spoken. I was in awe of it, and while some part of me craved that experience, it wasn't my time.

But now it was. I had signed up for a 10-day sit-in at a Vipassana center in Onalaska, Washington before I left New York. I knew it was my moment and probably the only time I'd have in my life to truly take a vacation from the world, to be completely by myself.

Before I could be alone, though, I needed to satisfy my deep hunger to be with my family. When my dad picked me up from the airport, I was overwhelmed with a sense of safety and belonging. I had been so ready three years before to leave it all behind to pursue my dreams, so never once did I imagine I would need home so badly.

That night, my dad and I sat at the kitchen table and talked for hours.

Sharing what had happened while looking into the face I knew and loved so well was like medicine. I knew he could help me carry the weight. I knew he would hear me and understand if not what I had been through, then the state of my heart.

When I lay down to sleep later that evening, my head on a familiar pillow, the constant noise in my mind had lessened to a buzz in the background. Sleep found me, and though I dreamed of fire and dust and smoke as usual, for the first time in months, I woke up looking forward to what lay ahead.

A few days later, I arrived at the Vipassana center, Dhamma Kuñja, in Southwestern Washington. Vipassana is a centuries-old technique meant to eradicate suffering. It's a method of mental purification that allows one to face life's tensions and problems in a calm, balanced way, an art of living one can use to make positive contributions to society.

The facility was clean, even though the architecture was older, and everyone welcomed me inside. Along with 40 other people, I sat in the main dining hall while the center's leaders shared guidelines and expectations. Our clothes were required to make no noise. Touching wasn't allowed, and neither was speaking, writing, music, dancing, or exercising. We were to meditate, eat, and sleep.

Our daily schedule was simple. Wake up at 5 a.m. with a gong, then meditate until 7 a.m. Enter the main hall, men on one side and women on the other, and after a short break, breakfast was served, followed by three hours of mediation. Lunchtime was from noon to 1 p.m, after which we were to meditate in our rooms from 1 to 2 p.m. and then from 3 to 5 p.m. in the hall. We broke for dinner from 5 to 6 p.m., free time from 7 to 8 p.m., then had a late meditation between 8 and 9 p.m.

They asked if anyone had additional questions, after which the silence began. It would not be broken for 10 days.

We were shown to our rooms, each one sparsely furnished with four beds. I picked a lower bunk, and the three other women found their spots. The room smelled of damp wood and pine.

I slept fitfully, and on the morning of day two, I was too tired to shower, so I changed and went to the main hall. There were mountains of big, flat cushiony pillows in orange, pink and red to relax on. The couple in the front of the room shared a breathing technique, then allowed us to follow them.

Comfort became my first priority. I needed to get my stomach strong to sit up and also relax my shoulders and my head. I worked to ground my frame, trying to find the ideal posture that allowed my head to almost float on my neck.

Once I found that spot, I started breathing. My mind was so loud in such a silent place that I wondered if the people next to me could hear all the chatter, the cacophony of thoughts ricocheting through my brain. I kept going from staying with my breath to focusing on the sensation of my breath around my nostrils to my mind's incessant noise. But I was reminded that we were to "remain equanimous," calm, composed, balanced, no matter what was happening inside our bodies or out in the world.

Gong...I made it! My first session of meditating for two hours, and I made it! I felt so strong. I felt so tired. I was ravenous, not just for food but for shared perspective. I longed to share my reflections with someone, but it would be over a week before I could.

On day four, I woke up earlier than 5 a.m. to take a shower and gather more strength. My legs ached, my body hurt, but I eased into the early morning session. When the gong rang, and I slowly got up, I started to think about my senses. At breakfast, taking small bites of the delicious vegan food, focusing on each chew, my actions were slow, intentional, and focused. I envisioned every part of the food nurturing me, giving me sustenance to be grounded for my next session. After the meal, the participants walked around each other, being patient with one another, using body language instead of words and tongues. In just a short time, we had learned to communicate without speaking.

During the next session, when we all gathered together in the main hall, I felt distinctly as though I was part of a larger organism. All these bodies, all these souls, we were here for the same purpose, breathing the same air, focused on the same sensations.

As I focused on my breath, on Anapana—the triangular space around the nostrils and the cupid's bow, the soft bit of skin above the upper lip—I was no longer caught up in the present. I was no longer thinking, planning, racing from one idea to the next. Instead, I felt memories wash over me. Me as a child, sitting on the floor, watching the dancing feet of friends and relatives. Me, older, floating in the water, looking up at a rare sunny Seattle sky. And then, a flash overtook my vision, and I saw the explosion that took my tower down. I saw fire all around me, as bright and as hot and powerful as if it were in the hall with us. *Equanimous*, I reminded myself, and the deeper I breathed, the more I could keep the flames at bay.

The daily routine started to create a new flow for us, and I started to see the connection between my thoughts and my feelings. If I closely monitored the why behind a feeling and followed the path it created in my body, where did that emotion reside within me?

When we do not watch, assess, and examine, when we react to our thoughts and emotions impulsively, we're actually making big valleys within. These valleys—the patterns of behavior, the ways in which we act that we are in fact trying to look at and for most of us change—are called *sankaras* and form every time you react to a particular situation in a particular way. With each choice, the valley deepens and widens, and slowly, slowly, it becomes more difficult to follow a different path. We are creatures of habit, after all.

Sometimes, an experience cuts so deep that it creates its own *sankara*. The memory took me over completely.

It was me picking up the phone to call Soriano. I hadn't talked to him since we broke up, but I had heard earlier that week that he'd been shot. I was newly in love with someone else, but I felt so bad for Soriano that I reached out. He picked up on the first ring and told me how much it hurt, how hard it had been. He asked to see me, and I said yes.

When I got there, we fell into the familiar rhythm of things, talking about life and catching up, and time passed too quickly. What he had said on the phone about his pain and difficulty didn't match with what I saw in front of me, but it was nice to see him. I felt reassured that he was alright, that enough time had passed since we broke up.

It was late, and I had to be at work in a few hours, so I asked if I could rest in the chair where I was sitting before heading downtown.

I nodded off. When I woke up, it wasn't to my alarm. It was to Soriano on top of me, inside of me, assaulting me. Raping me.

"No! Get the fuck off me!" I screamed, filled with fury and flame.

My eyes flew open, and instead of seeing the faded furniture of his apartment, I realized I was still in the main mediation hall. My heart threatened to beat straight through my ribcage. I stood up, breaking my sit and went outside.

I breathed the cold air deeply, taking comfort in the starless night. One of the volunteers came up behind me. I wanted to tell her. I wanted to tell her what the bastard did to me. How I never had—and would never have—hurt him. That I was always a good person to him. That I felt so stupid to naively think he and I could be friends, that sadness and empathy for him getting shot took over what felt like common sense.

My rage shone through me.

"Whatever it is," she said, looking me in the eye. "Remain equanimous."

I shook, tears streaming down my face. My mouth opened, the words, "But he…," on my tongue.

She interrupted me. "Go back in. Stay with your breath. Be equanimous."

I did as she said, the urge to scream, to explain dissipating as I took each step. What is there to discuss? It had happened. My clenched heart and fierce anger were my reaction to a past memory of abuse.

He must have no soul, I thought, perhaps to give me permission to focus on mine.

I sat back down, breathed deeply, and tried to let go of my thoughts. They bombarded me, so I recognized them and tried to remain still. I felt stupid for trusting him. I felt ashamed that I was there in the first place, that he had touched me, been that close to me, even though I had not given permission. I felt angry that this seemed to be a pattern in my life.

That was the third time in my life a man had sexually abused me. Five years old, 13 years old, 19 years old. I was so furious; every cell was blistering hot, steaming. I could feel the air on my upper lip even more now because it was moist with sweat. I was angry at the cumulative injustice but angry, too, for being a girl with low self-esteem, someone who chose a terrible person like Soriano, a person who never treated me well.

And perhaps angrier that, in this moment, during this time of healing and reflection, when I was supposed to be grappling with a near-death experience I had so recently endured, *this* was capturing my mental and body space. Why was this coming up so clearly and sharply in my body now? I realized that my body remembered this as fresh trauma and it was in watching my sensation in my body, that reminded me of what happened.

I pictured Soriano's ugly, pock-marked face, and I told him, *I did not come here for you. I came here for me.* I visualized instead the light in front of me and within me. I breathed with intention, in and out, in and out. Equanimous.

I felt around in my body, searching for the sensation that was the source of these feelings, of this shame. That was what I was there to learn: how to watch the memories, how they are connected to my physical body, and how to watch and not react and let them overtake my soul. Only then could I choose my response to memory. Only then could I find true peace with the past.

I searched my mind, my lungs, my limbs, but I felt the fire only between my legs. It was a shameful flame, a normal sensation that had taken on a dirty meaning. Instead of feeling that warmth in my *yoni* and equating it with love, sex, belonging, physicality, womanhood, and beauty, it now meant humiliation and anger. Observing those feelings down there made me remember being raped, but when watching myself replaying the memories of the moment, it was very clear to me: when he raped me, it was another experience that took the wonderful goodness out of love-making and out of my life.

Watching the dynamic between the mind, emotions, and between the body, my memory allowed me to unlock a secret. In life's darkest moments, prayer had always helped me. Praying was the place where God and I could be together, where I could be my true self. Music and dancing also helped to heal my spirits.

But when the towers fell, and I almost fell with them, all the tools I had to cope and connect with myself and the world had shattered. They were no longer enough. I hit a wall.

And now I had a new tool. All I needed was my own power, my own breath, to help me observe and regain control of my past and my future by being present. For the first time, I had a strong sense that I was exactly where I was supposed to be. Peace fell upon me, grew from within me. Strength radiated out from my center, and purpose pulsed through my veins. I felt God there within me. I felt it all.

That night when I went to bed, I cried, full sobs, wails that erupted from corners of me so long ignored. I cried for all the pain I had ever experienced from another, for the ways they abused me for my flesh, dragged me in the mud, held me back from my true self. I cried for all the time I wasted, feeling like I had no choice but to be broken. I cried for every moment I had spent not being able to love myself.

The morning came, and the sun was shining through all the windows, trickling through the drapes. The sun is so glorious after a dark night.

I breathed, then I breathed again, and stayed with my breath. That day in the hall was an exercise in humanity, in my own humanness. I could so clearly see the dynamic among my mind, my emotions, and my body. It came to me in the form of a triangle, such a simple shape and so capable of such inspiration. How could I have gone for so long without truly understanding what drives me, controls me, and sets me free?

The secret had been unleashed, and I was unencumbered on day seven. I could follow my breath; I could feel my nostrils. I loved how my concentration was so focused that when I would scan my body, I could truly feel it all.

I focused on different parts of my body. I scanned my midsection, then my stomach. My stomach was fully present, and when I visualized it, it vibrated a deep source of light. I could travel within it, exploring what it looked like, felt like. All I could do was stay there in that place in my body, feeling the glory within, the light and bliss! I smiled as a memory struck me: science class at Blanchet, the page of a textbook, a lesson about atoms. *Our cells, protons, electrons, neutrons are all made of energy.* Once a mere fact, I could now feel it to be true in a way I never thought possible.

I went back to my stomach and started wanting to feel it completely again. But now that I wanted it, the more I wanted, the more I was feeling less and less of myself. In my mind, all I could do was just want to be there, feel my desire to stay in that light and project it to other parts of my body. I wasn't watching anymore, but rather visualizing and desiring.

I thought to myself, "Have I ever felt this before?" And the memory returned, as clear as though I was back there on this day. The Church of the Good Shepherd, on Broadway and Isham, on September 11th, standing at the pew and praying for all the souls who had passed. I felt God that day, in the silence all around me, in all the cells within me. I felt the current of my blood flowing through my veins. I felt alive, truly alive, in a way I never had before. And here I was again. The first encounter was during the darkest moment of my life, the second during the most enlightened.

In the rhythm of life, when we're all caught up in the comings and goings, wrapped up in the minutiae and the mundane, we have no space for it, no time. For me, these two moments of clarity came at the poles of my human experience—so close to death, so committed to life—but they also both showed me so clearly that God is always with us. Through pain comes perspective. Through trauma can come truth.

In the Bible, Jesus said: "While you have the light, believe in the light, that you may become sons of light." I felt like a child of God.

I breathed. Then I asked myself, "Who else has felt this? Who else knows how they work inside?" Imagine the power we have when we do less petitioning, asking, wanting but remain in stillness and silence? We can move to "being" and completely surrender because we know God is with us all the time. Through trauma, through peace, I experienced the light, the life force, the omniscient, the almighty, Manna, the highest consciousness, the universe, God. Yes, God is truly always with us, but not only that. He is *within* us.

On the last day, we woke up late at 7:30 a.m. and were given our last meal, a delicious vegan breakfast. The silence was about to end, and we were reminded that, for some, sound would come as a shock to our system. Speaking, we were told, also takes a lot of energy, so they advised us to listen to our bodies, to take rests, and to plan on taking it easy as we re-entered the world.

I walked into the main dining area quietly and found some familiar faces—the other three women with whom I shared a room and another woman was sitting off at the next table. I was drawn to her bright smile and eyes. We spoke, and learned we were both from New York, just visiting this part of the world. She was from Trinidad and one of the few women of color there. We exchanged numbers and committed to visiting each other in New York. It was brief, because speaking was exhausting. I turned, and then one of the ladies in my room immediately embraced me. "My heart was ready to burst hearing you cry at night," she said. My name is Dalya.

"Thank you, I'm Annabel," I told them all.

"I almost leaped out to hug you so many times, but it was against the rules."

"I'm so sorry," I said, embarrassed. "I couldn't stop crying on some of those nights."

"It was so hard not to speak with you," she said. "But I noticed when you were sitting in front of me in the main hall, you stayed so still and sat up so straight. I was struggling but just seeing how strong you were even though I knew you were suffering was such an inspiration to me.

The other ladies chimed in, and said, "you were so still; you barely moved at all."

"Really?" I asked. It was one of the nicest compliments I could have been given after the time we had all spent together. "I'd never done this before. I just focused on my breath and tried my best."

"It was the best gift to us all," she said, and the other women nodded.

As we spoke, I could feel my energy getting used up, bit by bit. I hugged them all, using what felt like my last bit of strength, and stepped outside into the crisp, cool air. I caught a whiff of smoke in the wind from a far-off flame.

Breathe, I whispered to myself. *Just breathe.*

12

Mother Earth

I stood with my hands on the ferry railing, looking out onto the sound of the Salish Sea. The cloud cover was complete, but it wasn't raining, a mercy in Washington during late November. I was on my way to Indianola for the second part of my West Coast reunion trip—to visit my dear friend Carolyn and hopefully continue to mend.

Only a short time had passed since the 10-day sit experience, and I still felt its strength within me, the stillness it had imparted in my soul. I looked out onto the beautiful sound, the island shores visible far off in the distance. Carolyn, an Eastern Band Cherokee woman who was taught by Lakota teachings, had heard I was in the towers on September 11th and reached out to me.

"I have something that will help you heal," she had said on the phone before inviting me to participate in an *Inipi* ceremony, a sacred Lakota Indian sweat lodge ritual. Though I was familiar with the concept, I knew very little about the practice.

"It's a way to pray to the Creator," said Carolyn. "But it's also a rite of passage, a ceremony of rebirth. *Inipi* in Lakota means "to live again.""

The *Inipi* ceremony (*ini-* from *inyan*, rock + *-pi*, lodge) is one of the Seven Sacred Rites of the Lakota people that has been passed down through generations in order to purify its participants.

To live again, I thought, and something stirred within me, reaching out to spur me forward.

"I'd love to," I said, honored and touched, filled with questions but curious and committed to whatever may come.

And now I was on my way, the islands inching closer on the horizon. As I looked out onto the water, a seagull swooped into view. Throughout the years, my brothers and sisters have always been convinced that I could speak to birds. Oftentimes, it's a joke—a pigeon coming up to me in the park to ask me for crumbs, a sparrow landing as though to sing a song just for me. It is often said in humor, but there's something deeper to these interactions, just as with the crows on that Tuesday morning. My family identifies as Ecuadorian, but genetically I am 50% Native American, and at times I feel as though it provides me with a unique channel to all that is natural and divine. More times than I can count, one of my family members would call me to say something like, *I saw a falcon fly this way, or do this thing, or cross my path at this moment. Annabel, what does that mean?*

I don't always have the answers, but I do know there is a deeper meaning, a message to which we can be attuned. Watching that seagull, the way it rode the currents of air and seemed to float, I could sense the comfort of its own freedom, how at home it was in the wind. I longed for that lightness. I wondered if perhaps I might be on my way to it.

I didn't know exactly what the sweat lodge would bring—Carolyn had explained that there would be singing, praying, and a focus on connecting with spirits and Mother Earth. Once I got off the ferry, I made my way to the meeting place. I knew that there I would be joined by a dozen or so other people who were coming for healing of themselves, others, and Mother Earth.

I walked toward the group and immediately saw Carolyn, who folded me into her arms in the warmest hug. Tears sprang to my eyes, and I breathed in deeply, loving the embrace of my old friend.

Carolyn walked to meet the rest of the group, and I noticed a woman about my age. I was struck by the force of recognition.

"Aren't you Dalya?" I asked. "Didn't we just meet at Vipassana?"

"Yes!" she screeched, immediately hugging me. "I cannot believe you're here!"

"What are the odds?" I asked.

She winked at me, smiling. "What is meant to be, will be," she said. "Who do you know here?"

"Carolyn! We were both on the same board many years ago, and we've kept in touch since."

"Ah, wonderful! Have you ever done a sweat lodge before?"

"No, never. I have no idea what to expect," I replied. "Carolyn really feels it will help me as my soul grounds itself after the 11th."

She took my hands in hers. "She's right," she said. "You'll see."

"Hello, everyone!" said Carolyn, addressing the group. "We are going to split up in three cars and head over to my place. Once we get there, there will be a lot of work we'll need everyone's help with. We'll need to prepare the area by raking, removing fallen branches, stacking wood, and doing whatever is necessary to keep the area clean and ready for the ceremony."

The drivers put up their hands, and we took our backpacks and belongings and headed to our car of choice. The road to the house was winding and flanked by tall cedars. In a line, we turned into a long driveway, at the end of which was a cozy house, the entire setting perfectly charming. I got out of the car and breathed in—the air was clean and crisp, a verdant smell, the bouquet of the Earth itself.

Carolyn took us on a tour of the house and land. In the driveway, there was a wood-chopping area, then she walked us through the garage to the back porch and into the kitchen. We were going to need a lot of wood chopped, one for the fire outside the *Inipi* and the other for the house. For nourishment, we were going to make a stew. She showed us all the potatoes and carrots that needed washing and cutting. The living room was warm and had a wood stove.

"We need this fire going at all times, so we'll need someone to get it started, watch it, and then take turns to rotate with someone else," said Carolyn.

She showed us where the sweat lodge would be. It looked like a small dome, no more than 8 feet wide, almost like an igloo made up of tree branches and blankets. It was still being prepared, with a few people layering blankets on top of the structured branches. Carolyn joined them. They were sweeping the whole area to remove the old stones and get new ones for this new ritual. They also smudged every object that was on the altar right outside the sweat lodge, then smudged each person, tying prayer ties and flags. Smudging is a ritual in which dried sage and cedar are burned, with the smoke as a purification for both people and thoughts. Just one step from the entrance to the lodge were two forked sticks, representing the trees. A pipe was placed at the crux of the sticks, the entirety of which was placed on a mound of dirt shaped like a turtle that was the altar.

After putting more blankets on the dome, a woman used a cedar broom to clean everything in and out of the structure. It was a true team of people. Carolyn asked us to get settled and pick an area to focus on so we could eat in the nice warm home as they prepared the finishing touches of the lodge for us.

I busied myself peeling and cutting vegetables for the stew that had just started to simmer. It reminded me of cooking with my mother—chopping onions, tomatoes, and peppers, then watching her transform them into the most delicious meals I'd ever tasted.

Once everyone was done with their work, the ceremony began in the late afternoon. Carolyn began by saying words in the Lakota tongue. She sang a song and began additional smudging.

"The lodge represents Mother Earth and the womb, so when we crawl out at the end of the ceremony, we leave all our problems in the lodge with the Grandfather and Grandmother Stone People," said Carolyn. "We emerge reborn."

I was wearing a longish skirt and a loose long-sleeved blouse with no makeup on or any jewelry. I brought a towel just for the *Inipi* ceremony—any other clothing made the heat unbearable.

When we first entered, crawling through a small flap in the front of the lodge, it was warm inside, like being embraced by the Earth itself. We crawled in a clockwise motion at the door to honor the four directions, saying, "*Mitakuye Oyasin,*" or "*All my relations, all my ancestors, all my family.*" Crawling wasn't just a logistical necessity—the roof was far too low to stand up—it was to humble and remind ourselves that we are all related and equal. There was no space between us—we were knee to knee and shoulder to shoulder.

Carolyn explained in the house that if the ladies were on their moontime, which was a very sacred ceremony for women, they could pray and stay in her home to do so. It wasn't punitive; it was just the way the ancestors had done it in deference to a woman's natural rhythm, the reverence held for the sacred ceremony rooted the ancient process, from the ways we enter Mother Earth's womb to the order of who speaks.

Carolyn held an eagle's wing, on top of which was a plume of feathers, and she used the wing like a talking stick. It was given to her by her Lakota elder from the whole shoulder of an eagle. The legend she shared was from one of her teachers, Greg Red Fox.

The Creator created the universe, the moon and stars and everything on Earth, everything except the people, then looked down and said, this is all good; everything is going to have a name. The Creator named the sun, the moon, the star nation, named the one leggeds the tree people, named the four leggeds the creepy crawlies, named the finned ones, and the last nation to be named was the winged ones.

Everything got a name because everything is alive. The Creator asked, "Is there anyone who doesn't have a name?" After spotting a little crusty-looking bird in the grass, the Creator asked, "Why didn't you come forward for a name?" And the bird said, "Look at me. My wings are so small I can't fly; my beak and my talons are so short I can't even tear food. And my feathers are so ugly, I am pitiful." And the Creator picked up the bird, blew four times—whoosh, whoosh, whoosh, whoosh—and then spun around and let the bird go. As it flew up, the wings got wider, the talons got longer, the beak got bigger, and it turned into what we all know as an eagle.

As it flew over the highest mountain, it hit its tail and turned it white, and as it flew through the highest cloud, it hit its head and turned it white as well. And that became the most honored bird, not because of its size or ability to hunt and see from afar, but because it had the most humble beginning. That is the true medicine of the eagle—humility—the most highly valued trait in Native culture. Nobody is important alone, but you are important to something bigger. You are a part of that great circle of universal creation.

There was so much love, strength, and meaning to Carolyn's eagle wing; it was an honor to hold. She then showed us a beautiful drum and shared a song with us. Each item she held in her hand had a story that came with it, and Carolyn would explain its significance, the legends and lore associated with it. In Western culture, things are just things. But here, each of the objects is a sacred living being.

The drum, which had been handed down from ceremony to ceremony, was used in rhythm to teach us the verses of the chant. Afterward, she took the drum outside and came back in. We were singing, which evolved into us sharing the eagle wing. After the wing went around, and we were all able to pray, we started a chant.

The lodge was blessed with sweetgrass, and the first lava rocks were brought in—they are the stone people, the symbols of the ancients. Carolyn welcomed them and slowly poured water over each of the stones, the steam filling the air around us. As we chanted, it got hotter and hotter.

Each of us began to pray out loud, separate thoughts all said in unison. Prayers offered to draw on all the powers of the universe—earth, water, fire, and air. I knew this could be a transcendent experience, a unifier with nature, but I was unprepared for the sensation of breaking down the walls between me and the natural world.

I could feel the trees around us, the sources and filters of life, the givers of so much. They give us patience, give us oxygen. They hold up the land underneath with their roots. They give us shade, fruit, homes for birds, beautiful greenery to gaze upon. They are still, yet they stand upright and strong no matter what life, or wind, or weather throws at them. They sacrifice so much to give us shelter. They give their lives, the ultimate sacrifice of their long years, just so we can build our own homes by chopping them down.

I had gone so long without the embrace of the trees. My apartment in the Bronx felt as far from nature as one could get. Yes, there were parks and the few root systems that sprung up from under the concrete, but being here, being home, felt different.

And so I prayed for them, for the leaves and the branches. I was grateful for their wisdom, their love, their forgiveness. I prayed that they would always find ways to live, that they would always be there for us, giving us more oxygen to breathe, always unconditionally loving us and detoxifying the air for us. It was their function, I realized. It was with the essence of their being that they truly express unconditional love for us all. It felt like a revelation, and I was enveloped with it. I soaked in the wisdom, secure and pure in the knowledge that trees actually love better than any human in history has ever been able to.

I saw a vision: Manhattan before industrialization, before colonization, before humans took all the trees had to offer to build the greatest city on Earth. My heart broke for them; my prayers went to them. How and when had we decided that a fallen forest was more valuable than a standing tree?

With so much fire from the 11th, so many fires from my childhood, I have seen how buildings are a short-lived answer to shelter. I have seen apartments, decks, and now the Twin Towers burn down the way we trample down the trees.

But here in the lodge, I was one with the fire. I have been around this element so much in my life, I know that it can give so much to us as humans, but it can also take so much from us when uncontrolled. In my life, I have feared fire. I have tried to avoid it, but it seemed to not only stay in my life but alter it. In the lodge, I could feel a deep shift within me, moving from a place of fear to a place of understanding. Instead of running from it, I paused to examine my relationship with this element. Through listening to the wisdom of Native elders, I had learned there are many sides to all the elemental forces. Yes, fire had the capacity to destroy, but it also had the capacity to heal. Though there was so much I did not understand, I felt my heart open. Mother Earth was holding me in her womb, and my ego was dying off again; it was leaving my body there in that lodge.

The words we were chanting, though unknown to me, had been spoken countless times across generations. The drum, the steadiness of the rhythm, a voice for all the hearts beating together in that space. The heat, overtaking me, holding me together, cleansing me of all I had carried in with me. Mother Earth and the ways of my Native ancestors who had lived so I could live and experience this moment. The energy between it all, the unseen, the intangible.

It all healed me. The sweat lodge was a catalyst, a cauterizer searing and sealing my wounds, sizzling the torn parts of myself back together again.

When the ceremony was over, we crawled out of the exit one by one, and I collapsed in the cool air outside. A woman wrapped me in a soft towel, brushing my sticky hair back from my forehead. She told me all would be well, and I believed her.

Slowly, I was able to stand, walk, and make my way back into Carolyn's house. I changed from my towel wrap back into my long skirt and a loose shirt, taking each motion slowly, aware of the need to stay in the moment because my mind and body weren't quite ready to process all that had happened.

I went into the living room and saw Carolyn there.

"Annabel," she said, hugging me close. "Let's get some nourishment in you, then I want to show you something."

I was given a deep earthen bowl filled with stew, thick and savory. It reminded me of *casuela*, the Ecuadorian stew I grew up loving. Though the ingredients were different, they were both made with the intent to give life, love, and energy to those who consumed it. It was exactly what my body needed—salty, earthy, savory.

My belly full, my soul mended, my body lighter somehow—I was tired. Everyone else had left, back to their homes and to their own healing. I was spending the night to spend some more time with Carolyn. She came into the room and sat down next to me, a deck of cards in her hands.

"You've begun to heal," she said. "Understanding your animal medicine will help guide the rest of your journey."

"To where?" I asked.

She shrugged, smiling. "To wherever it is you're supposed to go."

Carolyn put the deck of cards down and a book next to it.

"Open it," she encouraged, and I obeyed, cracking the book's spine to reveal worn pages filled with wisdom. I read about animal medicine. In Native culture, it is believed that when a certain animal crosses our path, they bring a message and significance with them. Because we now live in cities and are not in nature as often as when we first walked the Earth, the cards have come to reacquaint us with our natural roots. The word "medicine" in Native American practice refers to the healing aspects that a particular animal brings to our consciousness—anything that gives us more context, more understanding, or that restores, strengthens, realigns, or revives the spiritual and physical body.

Carolyn shuffled the deck of cards.

"Pick one," she said simply.

I drew a card from the middle of the deck, showing it to her.

"Turn to that page," she prompted.

"The bat?!" I asked, incredulous. The bat always seemed to bring with it negative connotations in Western culture—darkness, death, and fear—the stuff horror movies are made of.

"Read before you judge," she offered gently, reading the description. "Bat medicine is powerful medicine. And perfect for this moment."

The pages described the bat as a gateway to new life and purpose, a symbol of rebirth in a time of darkness, of sloughing off the old life in favor of spiritual growth. It can be a scary transition, but if you can face that fear, you will walk into your new purpose with a strengthened intuition. The bat can help you transition into a new life. It will help you grow into your destiny and find the right future.

I was sitting up straighter now, the book's wisdom seeming to speak directly to my soul.

"I am ready for that," I said finally, holding an image of fire in my mind. It was no longer a source of fear, the flames from the towers threatening to engulf me from above and below. It felt now like a source of strength from the great spirit, as though armed with the potency of silence and breath and healed by the embrace of Mother Earth. What had happened to me didn't have to determine what would happen next. I felt free.

"Pick another card," Carolyn instructed.

I nodded and pulled a second card from the deck, flipping it face up. What looked back at me gave me goosebumps on every inch of flesh.

The crow.

I must have gasped because Carolyn asked, "What does this mean to you?"

"I keep seeing crows. It seems like they're everywhere," I admitted. "On September 11th, I woke up to the sound of them, just outside my window. They covered the whole tree, cawing at me, almost calling to me, it seemed."

We flipped to the page of the crow and read. Crows are omens of change, our animal connection with the spirit world.

"I have no doubt they were telling you that your life would be forever altered that day," said Carolyn. "Did you see them after September 11th?"

"Yes, they seem to follow me. Or maybe I am following them."

We kept reading. Crows are powerful messengers, flying between the worlds of life and death, carrying the energy flows of ceremonial magic between the ceremony and the intended destination. If a ceremony was meant to heal the land after a disaster or help a family in need, crows would be trusted to carry that courage, strength, and energy.

Crows are the keepers of universal law and often act to remind us of the magic of life that is all around us, to help us remember the difference between divine law and man's law. One of their biggest messages is that we are all connected, that the basis of universal law is, in fact, unconditional love. They are representations of creation and spiritual strength.

On the page was a short poem:

Are you cawing so I may know
The secrets of balance within my soul?
Or are you sending your sacred caw
Just to remind me of universal laws?

"That's exactly what I've been saying the past few months!" I exclaimed. "I've asked so many questions, and I keep coming back to exactly this answer, the division between man's laws and God's laws. And the presence of something that transcends them both."

"The crow has done his job then, I think," said Carolyn. "These animals are strong medicine for you, Annabel. Keep your eyes open, and I am sure they will guide you well."

On the ferry ride back the next morning, I once again found myself gazing out onto the water, a sliver of sunlight bouncing off the waves as I reflected on the experience I'd just had. I looked up to the lush green mountains, up further to the sky, across to the shores, and within to the effect Mother Earth had had on me.

How often, how many times in my life, had I taken Our Mother for granted? How many people walked along her surface, used up her resources, but had not stopped to admire her beauty? She does so much for us, more than we ever speak of or acknowledge.

It had to change. How could I better bless her, honor her? How could I deepen my relationship with her?

I had heard the call of the mountains, the call of the trees, beckoning me to come back to the West Coast, to my childhood home. I knew now they wanted me here to nourish me, to heal and protect me. To let me know that I always carry a piece of them with me no matter where I am. Just as wine is defined by the soil the grapes are grown in, so are our lives. Where we come from is always a part of who we are. Mother Earth's love was within me, always as deep as the roots of the cedars all around.

My Native roots and practices, these newfound deep beliefs, settled into me. They found space next to my Christian faith, filling the cracks that had formed throughout the years. Combined with my meditation, I felt spiritually whole for the first time in a long time, perhaps forever. These three pillars—Christianity, meditation, and Indigenous ways of relating—were the anchors I had long been looking for.

September 11th had unmoored me, and my spirit longed for something to hold on to, some purpose of which to be a part. I had found it here, among the trees and the mountains, in the belly of the Earth and in the simple power of my breath.

I returned to my dad's house, pulled into the driveway, and put the car in park. I closed my eyes, leaning my head back against the seat, inhaling and exhaling to silently mark the end of this particular journey. I was looking forward to spending time here before returning to New York, and I knew I'd miss it once I left. What would be waiting for me when I returned? How could I take these lessons with me and apply them to my daily life?

I heard a rustling in the trees and looked up. Not far from me, perched on the end of a branch, was a crow, his black head cocked to the side and a single eye on me. His message seemed clear: a reminder that whatever changes the universe had in store, I was now rooted in universal law and spiritual strength, the keys to navigating changes while staying true to myself.

"We'll do it together, won't we?" I asked him, grateful for the guide.

He cawed in agreement, and I stepped outside feeling stronger than ever.

13

A New New York

H ome. Just one word, but so many meanings. It was here, in my dad and Shirley's home. It was in the smell of my mother's cooking, in the creak of a church pew sitting next to my brothers and sisters. And in New York, the place that had inspired so many dreams and recently been the source of so much unrest.

Back from the island with Carolyn, back from my spiritual exploration, just being with my dad and Shirley was a true comfort. They wrapped me in their love and filled me with warm memories of all the joy from years upon years of gatherings and celebrations. This was always where our family came together.

I sank down into the familiar couch, the same couch that had held my younger self, my brother, my sister, my niece, and my cousins. I could feel their memories, almost sense the imprint of their bodies on the cushions. But at that moment, though I missed them, more than anything, I craved the company of a different companion.

My father came into the living room as though on cue.

"I remember," he said with his kind yet commanding voice, "I remember sitting here when you were younger, teaching you about quadratic equations and chemical equilibrium, reading textbooks together, getting you ready for tests."

"I couldn't have done it without you, dad," I said, which was true. My success in school had been stoked by his teaching and his constant attention to our studies. He was a brilliant man, naturally gifted in so many ways.

"I may have helped, but that was all you, Annabel," he said, "And look at you now... my college girl. My Wall Street whiz. But I worry about you shouldering so much and still determined to change the world."

He sat down next to me and took my hand in his. I had held his hands thousands of times, but now I took the time to consider them, to look closely: prominent veins, king-sized nail beds, a finger-width-stretch that could entirely encompass my own. My hand in his looked like a child's.

His own childhood had been short-lived. From a young age, he knew he wanted to immigrate to the United States from Ecuador, which meant either a ton of money or the armed services. He chose the latter, joining the Ecuadorian army. He took to it immediately and rose quickly up the ranks, but others were threatened by his success. They didn't like the smart, good-looking, light-skinned Ecuadorian getting all the attention and praise. The powers that be asked him to consider making the armed services his career, but he declined, disheartened by the treatment of his fellow servicemen and believing in the destiny he'd always pictured for himself: a quiet life in the United States surrounded by green and mountains and trees.

He settled in Seattle, and over the years, brought his two brothers and his mother to stay. They took courses and became US citizens, and together they lived lives with their feet in these two places, straddling Ecuadorian and American culture, but always grateful for the life they were able to build for themselves.

Growing up, the most common phrase we heard in our house was: "*Nosotros somos tan bendecidos.*" *We are so blessed.*

Today, sitting on the couch with him, our fingers intertwined, I heard it again.

"I am so blessed as a father to have you here," he began, but the words caught in his throat. "To have you here alive and well, to be able to cry here with you. Unfortunately, I know other parents are not so lucky. And I want you to know that if you ever want to come back home, for a few days or for the rest of time, just come back. We'd love to have you here with us."

He stroked my hair with his hand, and I rested my head on his shoulder. The tears came and would not stop.

"Everything just feels so cruel, dad," I said, not in response to any one thing, but rather the mindset that was condoned by so many. My time in New York had been so many things—exciting, surprising, a test of my mettle and my strength. But the challenges were real, and the energy it took to not just survive, but try to thrive, was immense. My skin had become thick, but my heart had become heavy.

Life in New York was unlike life anywhere else—the day-to-day experiences, the practices you adopt to be able to navigate that urban world and fellow man—it took an emotional toll. It was a constant assessment of surroundings, a continuous learning of street smarts. Every day was an energy exchange, an exercise in intuition. You have to be conscious of your own space. You have to determine in a split second whether or not the person across from you will be threatened if you make eye contact. The attention to your body, your mind, and your interpersonal practices is a constant drain. And if you don't care for yourself and prioritize your own feelings, no one else will. They're all too busy fending for themselves.

The comfort I felt in that moment, breathing in the familiar smell of my father's soap and the subtle scent of cedar flowing in from outdoors, was intoxicating. My muscles relaxed. My spirit felt more buoyant. Clarity crept a bit further into my mind.

"It feels so good to be home, dad. And I so appreciate the offer to stay," I said, drawing on a newly replenished resolve. "But I have to go back to New York. I haven't finished what I started. I can't let what happened hold me back from everything I know I can do."

"I understand," he said. "But if you ever change your mind, our home and arms are wide open for you."

A few days later, my bags were packed. My dad took me to the airport, we were both crying again, soft, silent tears that traced the contours of our faces with every blink. I gave my dad one last quick hug, afraid to hold on too long or I might never let go.

I grabbed my bags and I didn't look back. I couldn't focus on what had happened, on where I had been or what I had been through. I couldn't retreat into the familiar, no matter how much it called out to me. I was determined to not let one day determine the rest of my life.

And so I left, boarding a plane that took me across the country, loosely following the reverse path of the plane that had crashed into the building above me and changed the course of my life. When we touched down just outside the city several hours later, I felt no fear. I felt capable, confident, anchored in justice, love, truth, and imagination. I was more grounded than I had left, delicate but no longer broken.

My apartment was quietly waiting for me. I opened the door and felt immense gratitude, a wave of peace washing over me. I sat down and realized with certainty that I could not continue in the way in which I had been living. I would have to start over completely. With my office gone and my future path unclear, my life had reached its own Ground Zero.

In the morning, I would begin to rebuild.

I woke up expecting to hear the chattering of crows outside my window, but all I could hear were the quiet early morning sounds of the city. I made myself a cup of tea and began thinking about how I was going to make my way in this new world. I couldn't imagine going back into the financial sector. It brought up too many memories, and the frantic cab ride thoughts that followed the explosion stayed with me. It felt like a career in support of money alone was not what my rebirth was about, that God wanted more from me.

Using the skills I had learned in the 10-day sit and the sweat lodge, I embraced the stillness and looked within. I felt so alive and strong with everything I experienced back home and so blessed to have discovered these new corners of my body and spirit. The memories of quiet, of ancestors, of blood pumping through my veins—these were the thoughts that guided me. I rested, trusting myself to discover what was raw within me, what was in the process of healing, where I could find solid ground.

What was my soul saying when my mind was still? How could I use this renewed connection with my body to make my next move? How could I make money without compromising my progress? It was very clear that I'm just a spirit in this body on Earth for a short period of time, so what was I going to do with the time I had? I realized that I could change job sectors and had transferable skills, so I wanted to find out how I could do what I was really good at.

Later that day, I stepped outside for some fresh air, knowing a walk in the crisp, cool weather was a sure path to clarity. One of the buildings I passed had a job board outside of it, and one of the flyers caught my eye—an image of a strong, fit woman with the headline, *"Make your body work for you."*

I took it home and called the number. Equinox Gym was looking for personal trainers, and although I had never done that before, looking death squarely in the face meant a new opportunity wasn't an intimidating prospect. I applied and was hired. The days fell into their own rhythm. The facilities were new and beautiful. I learned something new every day, training to become certified, mastering new techniques, and studying for exams with the same vigor and hunger I'd used to try and master the markets.

During my days off, in the quiet of the morning and stillness of the evening, I spent my time deep in reflection. The frantic pace of life before September 11th had been replaced by an embrace of solitude.

I would wake up and thank God for the day. For the sun, for the squirrels, for the crows, and for my breath. I would sit and meditate. I would go for a run in Van Cortlandt Park, pick up some food to nourish my body, and come back to my apartment. Turning up the volume, I would blast classical music, letting the notes fill me up, infusing my body and space with necessary calm.

I felt each day as another passing that kept taking me further and further from the 11th. I had escaped a spiritual burning building, and everything after that, each small step I took, was pouring the spirit back into me. It was a rebirth. I knew with great clarity the nature of my life, —never ending expressions of my soul. That death was an inevitability, and I would only be on Earth for a short while. It didn't sadden me. It didn't stop me. Instead, it helped me keep my head in the present and my eyes on the future.

The year 2003 was a cocoon, the framework I needed to be able to break through stronger than ever and once again pursue my dreams. Every day, I found new strength and felt closer to once again embracing my purpose. I knew nothing would ever be the same, but I finally had faith that something good could replace it.

And almost on cue, I felt my cell phone buzz in my pocket the next day as I walked to get lunch on the Upper West Side. I didn't recognize the number, but ever since losing out on the modeling gig for Jay-Z, I always picked up when an unknown number called. And I was glad I did—this time, it was the photographer from my *Blaze* photo shoot, and she wanted to work together again, this time for *URB* music magazine. I was in. I told her I had a friend, Toofly, who was a dope graffiti artist, and soon plans were being made. The shoot was going to take place in a few weeks, and I was so ready.

It was the first thing I felt excited about in such a long time. When the day came, I was nervous, tentative, but also determined to give it my all. The shoot was focused entirely on female hip-hop artists: me; a girl I hadn't met; Ana "Rokafella" Garcia, a legendary b-girl; and TooFly doing murals against a white backdrop. It was all about bright colors, bold females, and celebrating the scene.

By the end of the day, I was relaxed and energized, filled with a renewed sense of purpose. This is what I had dreamed of. I had been knocked back, but I hadn't been knocked down. It was a resounding reminder that I had bigger plans.

I called the headhunter with whom I had worked to place me at Telligent hedge fund. It seemed like a lifetime ago, but when she picked up the phone, her familiar voice helped spur me forward.

"I'm ready to find work again," I said.

"Then let's find you something great," she replied.

My first interview was scheduled for an executive assistant position at a firm in Midtown. I arrived and double-checked the address, hoping I was in the wrong place, then looked up again at the huge skyscraper that towered overhead.

Anxiety bubbled up within me. I had stayed below the third story since the 11th, fearful of climbing too far up in case the world once again came crashing down. I could taste the fear, struggled to swallow it down, but I could not let it choke my ambition.

I walked up to the entrance and into the lobby, letting the receptionist know who I was there to see.

"Suite two," she replied casually. "41st floor."

I stepped into the elevator, pressed the button, and watched as the doors closed in front of me. After I exited the 41st floor, I found my way to the office, each step a conscious decision to not let the panic get the best of me.

I met the leader of the team, and we sat down in a conference room with a view of the city. I couldn't help but feel the space between me and the Earth, sensing the precarious nature of this man-made structure that so willfully defied gravity. Held up by steel pillars and concrete, the floor may have felt secure underfoot, but I knew in my bones that I wasn't on solid ground.

I kept my eyes on the man in front of me as he took out my resume, examining it line by line.

"Well, Ms. Quintero, I see that you do have some of the experience we're looking for," he said as I tried to remain calm and confident. "I do have to ask about this gap in your employment history, however."

"Yes, I'm happy to discuss that," I replied, keeping my voice as even as I could, hoping beyond hope that I wouldn't have to divulge the real reason. "What would you like to know?"

He looked closer at the page and then quickly up at me.

"Oh, wow. Oh, my," he said. "I see that your last position was at the World Trade Center. That must be the reason."

I nodded. He continued.

"Did they recover afterward?"

"They did, but I had a hard time. I was in the towers when we were attacked."

His face turned red. "I am so sorry," he said and nervously looked around. "My goodness, are you okay with being in a tall building like this?"

I flushed, and my eyes began to water. I felt the muscles in my neck tense, preparing to turn my head from side to side to say *no*. No, I am not okay. But I stopped.

"I'm all right," I muttered, though I was sure that he could tell that I wasn't.

His tone changed as he put kindness into each word.

"I so appreciate you coming here to discuss this position," he said. "It's a miracle to meet you. We'll be in touch."

The interview was over practically before it began. He walked me back to the elevator.

"I really hope things work out for you," he said.

"Thank you," I replied, managing a smile. "I do, too."

When I reached the ground level, I practically ran outside. I gulped in the cold air, grateful as it seared my lungs. Once I calmed slightly, I called the headhunter.

"I am not going to get that job," I said as soon as she picked up the phone. "I know this might seem strange, but for future interviews, I need to know the office location. I can't be in a tall building."

"Absolutely, Annabel," she said. "We'll make it work. Don't worry."

But I was worried. I wasn't used to being afraid of things. I wasn't used to having a response to a memory become so powerful that it stopped me, that it dictated what was possible for me. I was used to overcoming, to resilience, to rising above. But how can you rise above, even metaphorically, when you're traumatized by heights?

Just breathe, Annabel, I heard a familiar voice say in my mind. *It's going to take you time.*

I felt so ready to live my life now, so proud of all the work I had done to create a new normal in which I could process my trauma and pain. I thought I was in a stable place. I thought I was ready. But all it took was one elevator ride to remind me that I still had further to go.

I jumped in a cab, and instead of asking the driver to take me home, I asked to be taken to the Cloisters via the West Side Highway. I felt the need to be in the presence of beauty and God, to be reminded of the bigger picture after feeling so trapped in my head. I walked around the Cloisters, marveling at the old monastery, then walked along the edges of Fort Tryon Park before peeling off to Broadway. As I continued toward the Bronx, I found myself close to the same church I had visited on the afternoon of September 11th, the Church of the Good Shepherd.

I remembered how I felt inside the last time I was there—feeling my heartbeat pulse in my veins, realizing my oneness with God and the universe, the gratitude for being alive and the guilt of surviving.

As I approached the church, a structure caught my eye. On the side of the huge stone structure was something new: a cross, unlike any cross I had ever seen. It was rusted, industrial, devoid of the ornamentation that usually accompanied religious artifacts.

I waited at the corner until cars passed, transfixed. I crossed the street, and with each step, I became more sure of what I was seeing. The cross stood as a monument, and the two pillars used to create it were steel beams, the metal singed, the corners twisted. They were from Ground Zero.

As I neared, I saw smooth gray stones surrounding it, each with a name, some with a picture. These were Inwood's firefighters that were lost in the towers. Each headstone was nestled into a carefully curated garden, the cross at the center.

I stood before it and looked up to the sky. I traced the oxidized metal with my finger, wondering: Was this beneath my feet when the planes hit? Was this beam supporting the stairs I used to *step, step, jump* to the sure ground below?

"Wow," I said in complete wonder. "You truly are here all the time, aren't you, God?"

As I walked home, I realized that things would have to change within me if I wanted my life here to work. First, honesty with myself, always. Second, just do the next right thing. Third, listen to the worlds within and the wisdom all around.

I knew I wasn't ready for corporate life. I knew I didn't want to work in a gym for the rest of my days, either. I loved modeling, but it was hard to make a mark. What fueled me? What sustained me? What was I truly passionate about?

I came home and sat quietly, letting thoughts come and letting thoughts go. I reached for the small bottle of scented oil I kept near my bed, casting out a few drops and rubbing them on my hands and pressure points. I loved the scent—*rain*—because it reminded me deeply of home: the rain-soaked Pacific Northwest, specifically a small shop in Seattle's Pike Place Market, Tenzing Momo.

I allowed myself to wonder about what it might be like to work there. The owners always seemed so happy, welcoming customers in and sharing the magic of tinctures, compounds, and herbs. I had always been fascinated by Eastern medicine, confounded by the capitalistic approach to wellness and the injection of so many toxic chemicals into beauty products and, by extension, into our bodies.

I inhaled deeply, calmed by the subtle perfume, and thought maybe this could be the next right thing for me. Instead of having to sacrifice my own health and healing in the name of work, perhaps I could make a living this way instead?

Energized, I dove immediately into creation mode. As I looked into the history of essential oils, I discovered that they, like me, had African roots. I researched the health benefits of antioxidant-rich almond oil, which had its own cultural roots. Almonds had been traded along the Silk Route from China to the rest of the world. In Africa, they became symbols of fertility. In the Middle East, they were a prized food. In almost every country, they had become lauded culinary and cultural staples.

And so I launched Lozi Lifestyle, a natural body oil brand that borrowed its name from the African culture—*lozi* being Swahili for almonds. Any time I wasn't training, I was working on the creation of the oils, crafting the perfect mix. When they were ready, I'd host get-togethers to share the history of *lozi* and their benefits.

The business took off, and soon I was making money while I marched closer to feeling whole and fulfilled. The buzz built, and soon I was approached by Ket, a dear friend in the culture and also a Director at Indigo, a big blue jean brand. They wanted to partner with me on a promotional spread. I agreed, and then came the best news of all: not only did they want to interview me as an entrepreneur and rep my products, but they also wanted me to model in the shoot as well.

I had found my way to another modeling gig, this time by honoring my purpose and trying to forge my own path. The shoot was everything! Mini jean skirts, forearm-length gloves, hair, heels, and even fake nails. I expected to have a good time, but what followed was a complete surprise.

Afterward, everyone on set was headed out for dinner and drinks, and they asked me to join them. I almost declined—I hadn't been out in so long. I had been so focused on building my business and prioritizing self-care that I hadn't been socializing. But there was a spark in me that I recognized, a small ember of freedom and joy that had been muffled for so long.

I said yes, and out we went, all of us together, some old friends and some new. The music was loud. The drinks were strong. The food was delicious. And the spark I had felt earlier exploded, fanned by the pure experience of just being young in the city. I could feel the vice grip that had held my heart loosen. Laughter followed. Joy poured in. For the first time in a long time, I was filled up with positive energy. I remembered why I had come all the way east in the first place, pulled to this coast like a moth to the flame. That night, I felt the power of the dream I refused to give up on. That night, I felt alive and unafraid.

Once more, I had been transformed by the magic of New York.

That small sliver of life and light cracked open the hard shell that surrounded me, fused together to protect me after the towers had fallen. Each day brought new momentum, small changes that came together to create a fulfilled existence I could proudly call my own.

After the winter had passed, on the first warm day of spring, I received a call from Indigo Red.

"There is something you've *got* to see, the billboard is up on 125th street" he said.

My curiosity piqued, my mind reeling at the possibilities. I dropped things, and took the train down there.

As I finally got towards, Lenox there it was. My billboard larger than *life*, Annabel."

I thought there must be something going as Paul was starting his new job; he had just started working at the Harlem Empowerment Zone on 125th. Kids just out of school played in the street, skipping over jump ropes, chasing each other and laughing. I felt grateful for the sunshine on my face.

I looked up.

I scanned for planes, a holdover from the 11th, always on the lookout for another attack. But the sky was clear with the hopeful, bright blue of spring.

What I saw instead was my own face looking back at me, as tall as 10 women, plastered against a billboard on the top of my brother's office building. I could not believe what I was seeing. It was more than the pure marvel of this colossal image. Tears sprang forth as I realized everything this picture, this moment, this achievement, represented.

Instead of being scared to stand in a tall building, my face was now at the top of one scraping the sky. Instead of being terrified of heights, I had risen to a new level.

I looked up again at the billboard, imagining my brother's voice on the line.

"Can you believe it, Schnannabel? You made it! You really made it."

Tears of joy threatened to spill down my cheeks. The mile-high Annabel was looking down at me, all confidence, grace, and swagger. She was on top of the skyline I used to trace in my childhood bedroom, dreaming of who I could become in the city that never sleeps. Only now the twin towers were missing, and there I was, strong and proud in their stead.

Perched at the topmost corner of the billboard was a familiar black figure, its wings outstretched, its head tilted my way. The beautiful crow cawed to me as if to say, *I told you so.* As if to say *we were on the right path all along.*

I stood there, strong and proud of not having given up. Despite having endured such a horrific nightmare, or perhaps because of it, my dreams had finally come true. I had lived through the worst terrorist attack in United States history. But I did not suffocate in the ashes. I didn't crumble in the ruins. September 11th had tried to destroy me, and in the process, I grew stronger. It had tried to bury me, but I discovered a truth: I was a seed. I grew upward from the flame-scorched ground like a phoenix rising from the rubble, my spirit reborn and my life remade.

Epilogue

September 11, 2021 marks the 20th anniversary of one of the greatest tragedies in living memory.

Although this book officially began with an email to my family in 2001, throughout the years I found solace in writing down my thoughts and memories, and in digging deep into the pain, frustration, and unceasing love I have for our future on this earth.

In the years since the planes knocked those buildings out of the sky, I continued upon my journey of self discovery and growth, finding moments of great joy counterbalanced with times of overwhelming despair. Such is the tapestry of life.

Each and every day since the towers fell, I feel its weight in my world. The pressure to make every day count, the guilt I felt in surviving but not yet having learned to thrive, the self-imposed silence I suffered through. To speak of that day in any ways other than a whisper or a prayer seemed like an injustice to those who were lost.

It wasn't until 2018 that I told anyone beyond my inner circle about what happened to me on that fateful fall day in New York City.

I had just begun the midlife search for more, the halfway point of reckoning that seems to happen to so many. I found myself looking for ways to add more meaning to my life, to deepen my purpose, and rekindle my journey toward growth. That process led me to a true mentor and teacher, Lisa Nichols, a prolific and transformational leader known for her fearless embrace of self love and integrity. Her teaching and wisdom spoke to me, and for the first time I was reminded of the power of investing in myself, and all the possibilities inherent in just being lucky enough to be alive.

After a particularly powerful development conference, I felt the pull of my trusty deck of animal spirit cards, the same methods and mythology I had learned just after my transformative experience in the sweat lodge. I placed nine cards on the table—my friend the bat had come to visit me in the eastern position. This meant it had a message for me for my spiritual path.

The bat signals rebirth, a breakdown of all the former notions of self in order to rise renewed and become my future. Its inverted position symbolizes the transposing of your former self into a newborn being. What I read helped me to finally understand why I had experienced so many different traumatic events throughout my life, not just September 11th but also so many smaller setbacks and tragedies.

Whether or not you believe in that magic, the bat's message proved to be prophetic in my life. Shortly after that, I was invited to speak on the Lisa Nichols stage and share my story with the world. After having spent years in the shadows of my own grief, trapped in the silence of a secret I kept out of survivor's guilt, I stood on stage in front of thousands of people and said these words out loud: *My name is Annabel Quintero and I am a September 11th survivor.*

I asked the audience: "How many of you have an untold story? How long have you been silent?"

A sea of hands reached for the sky.

That experience changed me. Instead of running away from tragedy—*step, step, jump*—I knew it was time to run towards my future with the same measure of force, energy, and speed.

This is why I am here. To take you on your own journey, so that you can take a deep emotional dive into your own experience, so you can reconcile your own blocks and trauma. And most of all, so you can find the power within you to speak your untold truth. Writing this book has evolved my healing, like medicine heals the body. We never truly know how much silence traps us and our true message, and our light is never truly experienced for all to see and feel. Just like in the ways we learn about ourselves, understand patterns and take new action to grow, that too is how we will evolve our society and this world. We are not separate from our history. It is as beautiful as it is painful. To know it and acknowledge it informs our collective patterns, so we can understand how we got to this present moment. When we understand structures and old mindsets then we can co-create a new systemic response and contribute to our collective consciousness and experience.

I hope these thoughts and lessons can provoke us to create:

Your life is yours alone. Allow regrets only to motivate you forward to fulfill your dreams.

Dancing heals—don't ever underestimate what somatic motion can do for you.

Share what is coming up emotionally with self-care, sometimes you end up exploding at the worst time simply because you kept it bottled up inside.

When you ask God or your higher consciousness a question, believe what comes up. And since you asked, heed the answer even if you are filled with fright.

In a crisis, if you don't know what to do, stop and breathe. Connecting with the sacred through your breath can save your life, or at the very least, give you data to make the next best decision.

There are all kinds of traumas and healing is cyclical.

Spiritually embark on that journey on your own.

Our history is beautiful & ugly, but to understand the present you have to know the past.

Knowing old mindsets and old decisions, helps you know what to change so you can create a new future.

Humans create ideas and babies; everything is else is given to us by Mother Earth.

You can be faithful and still tease out what is not loving from your faith.

Being critical of your faith and seeing where old thinking like colonialism still resides and where cultural dominance remains, is necessary to grow.

If multi-national companies could pay a global minimum wage, how would that impact our world?

If our commodities market could invest a % of a basis point for Mother Earth; so Mother Earth can also profit from her own resources how would that impact us?

Your intuition is your superpower.

If you hit rock bottom, when all the normalcy of your life is gone and you only have the shell of your skin: you are both enough and everything at the same time. Remind yourself, "I am a Soul experiencing life in this vessel." Your spirit is more powerful than any condition or circumstance.

Your mind is powerful, when emotional overwhelm comes up, distract it by serving others.

Being knowledgeable is not the same as being wise, let your wisdom be your wealth.

Your personal growth and healing contributes to the collective experience and consciousness.

"Don't misuse your imagination with worry." The mind can trap you or set you free, go higher in your consciousness beyond your five senses and see how everything begins to change.

That as we understand the injustices of our world both past and present, we can feel the depth of someone else's pain and allow our compassion to move us to take new action.

Your enemy might just be you. You may not know what your silence is condoning, nor that your ignorance might be colluding with the problem.

That God is much more integrated within us than we allow ourselves to experience, that we are not separate from God, just like we are not separate from our government or our history. We are the church, we are the friend, we are the enemy, and we will be the ancestors.

There is always wisdom in your life-altering event. There is always a lesson in the pain, a lesson of what we can learn from each other during the hardest moments of our life.

Your trauma can be transmuted into your triumph.

Your story and how you give it voice can accelerate someone else's healing.

My hope in sharing this story is that you begin to compassionately do your inner work. Step one, understand yourself by acknowledging your cultural blind spots, blocks and traumas. Step two, practice self-awareness, watch your own mind and choose your responses. After the first two steps, you know yourself and know what isn't working, so don't give your mind a moment to get filled with fright or comfort. Instead, you simply have to take new action and jump forward into the unknown.

Step for peace within our hearts, step for peace within our minds, and jump for peace within our bodies so that we can heal and contribute to the collective experience holistically.

I hope that this book allows everyone to understand Latino history in a way that humanizes us, that allows one to understand that we as an ethnic group are a history of multi-racial experiences of the Western hemisphere, we are American history.

I hope that my can contribute to our humanity, as we still contribute to the healing of our collective traumatic events. Women of color in America feelings and thoughts rarely become part of the collective dialogue. I hope we all find the bravery and honesty to confront the internal heartbreak we dare not share in our classrooms and offices, being courageous is being vulnerable. Our vulnerability is our strength and resilience.

I hope I have done my ancestors justice in sharing their history. I hope I have helped to shed light on the generational trauma that too often goes unspoken and unacknowledged.

In my present-day work as a holistic mindset advisor, I share my stories and lessons to inspire clients to thrive, to make the most of this moment, and always to know we are more than our current circumstance. I help leaders examine, understand, and embrace their whole selves in the name of the greater good. If you are ready to soar but are at a plateau you just can't get through or even helping those trying to escape their own spiritual burning building, I guide you through to your breakthrough.

As a cultural broker, I am committed to redefining what society means, and to help us individually and collectively discover how we define wellness. As a coach, I guide you through your own inner work so that you too, can share your story, so that you have the inner tools and the inner wellness for your future self, for the dream you are stepping into. If you are ready for more in your life? If you are tired of staying silent, or if you are a leader who wants to fully embrace everyone's wellbeing, contact me at www.stepstepjump.com.

My name is Annabel Quintero and I am a September 11th survivor.

But I am so much more than that. I am an evolutionary monument to the fallen. I am a friend to the crows and a believer of saints. I am a city girl who is at home in the stillness of the trees. I am a child of the earth and a lover of life. We are far stronger than we ever believed possible. We have this day to make it count in so many ways. So, are you ready?

Step, step, jump.

Acknowledgements

Thank Mom and Dad for being the first in your families to come to the United States on your own. You both were young pioneers in your respective families, and you opened up your home and paved the way for our Quintero and Ortiz families to have a better life. It is in your resourcefulness, hard work ethic, and faith that gave me a grateful perspective for those who take risks.

To Paul, Norma, Johanna, and Carol thank you for all the beautiful memories, for seeing through the hard times, and always keeping honesty and love between us. As the youngest, I have learned from you all, and your life inspired me to do more with mine.

To Sophia and Selene, you two are such strong loving girls. I can't thank you enough for holding me when I would cry, for seeing me as a person, not just your mom and mostly for being you. I learn so much for your creative and sweetheart Sophia and so much from your questions Selene. You both are like two parts of myself, and I couldn't have reached this moment in my life without being your mother. Being able to be your mother has been so special to me, thank you my goddesses.

Veronica Garcia, thank you for holding space for me, and letting me be the humble girl you know me to be. Thank you for being such a bright light of hope for me, for making me laugh, and for all the love.

Lauryn Chavez, thank you for asking me to model back in 2017, it truly opened me up so much. You love me for me, and allow me to be my beautiful self, and that has made such a huge difference in my transformation to come back into my own.

Dr. Allyson Gonzalez, thank you for being such a dear friend. Thank you for being such a dear friend, and holding space for me throughout this journey. I appreciate the way you pour into me, because your mindset is brilliant and so so beautiful.

Reverend Joanne Colemen, thank you for walking this journey with me. I love how we share our wisdom and lessons in our conversations about spirituality. Most importantly, thank you for being so inspired after me sharing my story with you, that you went straight into a rhythmic iteration with step step jump during Lisa's speak and write. You are such an amazing orator full of song, knowledge, and poems thank for sharing your gifts with me.

Ashley Rappa, my dear friend. Thank you for holding my hand, for asking me those questions, for all the conversation throughout this journey. Sharing my story with you on such a personal basis, the tears, and the emotional ride, I truly couldn't have done it without you. You are the most amazing book coach and editor, and you really put your all into hearing me and helping me during the most difficult times. Thank you for guiding me and bringing my story to life to share with the world. So grateful for you.

Carolyn Hartness "Heartness", thank you for inviting me to the sweat lodge 20 years ago. You knew it would help heal me and I am so grateful how you respectively teach and help me grow. Thank you for opening my eyes to indigenous ways of being and being a grounded source of light in my life.

My SAC Coach tribe, thank you for supporting me and being together during this journey.

Twyla, Pamela, Angela, Maria, Trina, Tamara, Dr. Sue, Dr. Virginia, Anjue, Shuntel, Carla, Tam, Stacey, Carrie, Erika, Tara, Christy Z, Jojo, Rainbow, Ashera, and Mari thank you ladies for being dear friends to me and supporting me through my life.

Lisa Nichols, thank you for giving me an example of what is possible in my life. The moment I stepped on your campus, you breathed life into my dream of becoming an author and sharing my story. The community you built, the lessons and tools you teach, have transformed my life. It is an honor to be part of the tribe as a Speaker Advocate Coach for your program. You were the only transformational coach who offered digital access to your conference, I signed up for Speak & Write in the fall of 2018. I made a plan and came to San Diego the spring of 2019 and then in Newport, CA in the fall of 2019. I had just graduated from the Ignite program, and was a selected speaker on your stage to share my story with the world! That moment changed something inside of me, and I haven't looked back since. God bless you always for making this journey an experience I didn't have to do alone. I wouldn't have met all the beautiful souls that support me today and that guided me and that are dear friends of mine and colleagues. Thank you for being that light, for helping me see a part of myself that needed to open up and truly shine.

Grandmother LaneSaan Moonwalker thank you for your wisdom and for sharing it with the world. You opened another up a whole other realm of understanding.

Dr. Rosa Meza thank you for your grace and grounded presence, your collective has allowed my truths to find confirmation and resonance.

Further Readings

Beckert, Sven. "Empire of Cotton." *The Atlantic,* theatlantic.com/business/archive/2014/12/empire-of-cotton/383660/. Accessed April 5, 2021.

Bennett, Lerone, Jr., 1928-2018. *Before The Mayflower; a History of the Negro in America, 1619-1964.* Baltimore: Penguin Books, 1988, p. 224.

Britannica, The Editors of Encyclopedia. "Tahuantinsuyu." *Encyclopedia Britannica*, 18 Jun. 2009, britannica.com/place/Tahuantinsuyu. Accessed May 4, 2021.

Bucheli, Marcelo. "Multinational corporations, totalitarian regimes and economic nationalism: United Fruit Company in Central America, 1899-1975." 2008, p. 545.

Carson, David & Sams, Jamie. *Medicine Cards.* St. Martin's Press; Revised edition (July 30, 1999).

Flood, Joe. "Why the Bronx Burned." *New York Post,* nypost.com/2010/05/16/why-the-bronx-burned/. Accessed April 5, 2021.

Herrera, Jack. "Mexico Asked Spain to Apologize for Its Conquest. Spain Said No." *Pacific Standard,* psmag.com/news/mexico-asked-spain-to-apologize-for-its-conquest-spain-said-no. Accessed March 26, 2019.

Ricciulli, Valeria. "'Decade of Fire': New Documentary Examines '70s Fires That Plagued South Bronx." *Curbed NY*, ny.curbed.com/2019/5/3/18525908/south-bronx-fires-decade-of-fire-vivian-vazquez-documentary. Accessed April 5, 2021.

"The American West: An Eclectic History: Differences Between British and Spanish Colonization of North America: Analysis of J.H. Elliot's Empire's of the Atlantic World." theamericanwestaneclectichistory.blogspot.com/2012/11/differences-between-british-and-spanish.html. Accessed March 12, 2013.

The Holy Bible, King James Version, Book of Revelations 18:19.

Todorov, Tzvetan. *The Conquest of America: The Question of the Other*. New York: HarperPerennial, 1992.

Weatherford, Jack. *Indian Givers: How the Indians of the Americas Transformed the World*. New York: Fawcett Columbine, 1990.

About the Author

Born to Ecuadorian parents and raised in Seattle, Annabel Quintero is a holistic mindset coach who believes we are all citizens of the world. Her diverse experience as a leader, educator, and entrepreneur are connected by a common thread: positively impacting people's lives. Whether she is Her own life was irrevocably changed on September 11th, 2001 when she narrowly escaped from the 46th floor of the World Trade Center's Tower One during the deadliest terrorist attack on U.S. soil. Ever since that day, she has devoted herself to empowering people and advancing the world around her through community engagement, continuous learning, and championing social change. In 2018, Annabel was on the ballot for the Washington State Senate, and is currently the owner of Step Step Jump, a personal development & wellness company dedicated to strength through healing that helps others optimize their health and reconnect to their true power. She is a lifelong b-girl, model, advocate, speaker, writer, coach, healer, mother, and lover of life.

If you're interested in booking me for a speaking engagement, coaching or leading a workshop for your company or organization, feel free to contact me here:

Linkedin: linkedin.com/in/annabelquintero

Facebook: https://www.facebook.com/annabelquintero

Instagram: @stepstep_jump

Website: www.stepstepjump.com

CPSIA information can be obtained
at www.ICGtesting.com
Printed in the USA
BVHW071706180621
609899BV00003B/335